AF149458

The Little Book
For Teachers
Who Think Big

Jeffrey Dutt, BSW, M.Ed

The Little Book
For Teachers
Who Think Big

VITA HISTRIA

Vita Histria

Las Vegas ◊ Chicago ◊ Palm Beach

Published in the United States of America by
Histria Books, a division of Histria LLC
7181 N. Hualapai Way, Suite 130-86
Las Vegas, NV 89166 USA
HistriaBooks.com

Vita Histria is an imprint of Histria Books. Titles published under the imprints of Histria Books are distributed worldwide.

All rights reserved. No part of this book may be reprinted or reproduced or utilized in any form or by any electronic, mechanical or other means, now known or hereafter invented, including photocopying and recording, or in any information storage or retrieval system, without the permission in writing from the Publisher.

Library of Congress Control Number: 2022943055

ISBN 978-1-59211-173-2 (hardcover)
ISBN 978-1-59211-245-6 (eBook)

Copyright © 2022 by Histria Books

Table of Contents

Introduction 7

Part I: The Landscape 15

    Today's Educational Environment 17

Standardized Testing 26

    Academic Diagnosticians 34

    Online Versus Traditional Education 43

Part II: Effective Teaching 51

    Characteristics of Effective Teachers 53

    Developing Creativity in the Age of Standardized Testing 62

    Dealing with Disruptive Behavior in the Classroom 72

    The Teacher as a Classroom and School Community Leader 90

    Don't Leave Anything to Chance 98

    Teachers Need to Be Effective Communicators 107

Part III: The Teaching Life 113

    The Balance 115

    What Can Society Do to Make Teachers Successful? 122

    Magical Moments 132

Appendix 143

Acknowledgments 145

About the Author 147

Introduction

I remember the day I walked across the stage at Lehigh University to accept my diploma in Special Education. The bold script on the piece of paper I had worked so hard for symbolized my years of effort. I was proud and idealistic, but as they say, timing is everything. A few months from taking the big leap into marriage, I chose to pursue a career in social work and business because the idea of teaching seemed too far removed from my life at that point. I was also young and impatient, and paid little attention to my talents.

As most teachers tell their students. Pay attention.

While my degree in education rested quietly in its glass frame, I struggled in my career, floundering from one job to the next, never quite finding my place. All I found was failure and frustration. For years, I was searching for a path that would fit my talents, my personality, and my desire to make my own decisions. Mostly, however, I wanted to leave my mark. While this sounds like the ultimate cliché, for me, it was true.

In 2002, a few weeks before Christmas, I lost my job as an admissions director for a local nursing home. I felt lost and distraught. At this point in my life, this had become a pattern, indicative of my struggle to find my place. I needed a job quickly because I was not bringing in any income. Knowing that substitute teaching would bring in steady income, I drove to the closest school district, the one I knew would have the most openings. In the human resources department, I filled out the appropriate paperwork and while waiting for the next hoop to jump through, the secretary of human resources cryptically said, "Wait a minute." She left the room, spoke to a man in another office, returned and asked, "Are you available for an interview right now?"

An interview? Right now?

Unable to believe my ears, I answered in the affirmative and followed her into his office. Miraculously, three hours later I was offered a job to teach in a Special Education English classroom the following January, right after Christmas vacation.

I was finally going to get the chance to do what I always wanted to. The seed planted during my adolescence was about to burst through the soil. The words of my former Sunday school teacher, Dale, came immediately to mind. Dale was an older man in his 60's when I first met him when I was 13. He was a friendly man, who despite having several different health issues, arrived each Sunday to teach his class. No matter the weather, personal issues, stress, or any other excuses, Dale was there in church to teach me every Sunday. Sometimes I was the only one in his class, but it didn't matter. He was there. We discussed life together, relationships with girls, and talked about the Bible and how it brings meaning to our lives. One snowy Sunday morning in January of 1982, Dale made a statement that has remained with me into adulthood, "The key to anything that you do in life is to form relationships." Many years later as I started teaching, I never forgot that advice, and I took it with me into the classroom.

Family and friends who are not in the teaching profession ask me often how I reach out to my students to teach them effectively. The key to a lot of what is illustrated in this book is based on forming those relationships with our students, effective teaching techniques and planning, and thinking on your feet.

No teacher can say that every lesson they create catches every one of our student's attention, but I did learn that getting to know your students and incorporating their interests and experiences into your lessons creates a classroom atmosphere that provides them with stability, creativity and fun. We usually forget about the fun because we concentrate on providing the students with the lesson components along with keeping control of our classroom. In speaking to many different teachers in the past couple of months, I realized that forming those relationships and being effective allows a teacher to be creative in their classrooms. Many of the professionals that I have spoken to bring up the aspect of teaching that we are lacking in our classrooms today. Teaching is split into two different categories, the science of teaching and the art of teaching. We should have programs that can evaluate how well students do in a scripted program with a test at the beginning and end of the program, as well as evaluation which is needed for future change or adaptations for students who struggle with the material. But, in reality, the area that is missing is the art of teaching. The art of the delivery is where we connect our academic lesson in a way that enables our students to become attentive and engaged to the lesson. We have so many scripted programs now that teach the subject matter, but these programs do not make the subject matter come alive. What does a scripted program look like?

One year, I was teaching reading to a 9th grade English class that struggled with vocabulary and comprehension. I had a scripted program called "Success for All," which was a program to help targeted students to become better readers and to comprehend what they had read. Most of my students in the classroom, about 25, had varied reading and comprehension levels. Some did not speak or comprehend English very well as they were native speakers in Spanish and Arabic. Most of my students' reading levels ranged from 2nd grade to 5th grade. They were not ready for the suggested readings in our 9th grade offerings including "Romeo and Juliet" and "Night." It would be futile to try and read these books with them because they could not comprehend the author's message nor could they possibly understand the words or context of the book.

As a new teacher it was suggested that I use the "Success for All" program to help my students increase their reading and comprehension levels to attempt to read the required books for their 9th grade English class. And, of course being a new teacher, I was ready to try something new as it seemed like a simple enough program to help my students. I set up the classroom to use this program. At first it seemed to work well because once the students saw success in what they were doing they became more motivated. However, as time went on the students became disinterested in the stories and the lessons that were included with the program, and consequently, bored. I was astounded!! I felt like there was a lot of empirical data that supported the program and its effectiveness, and I was impressed with the scientific data that was available to back up its merit. Although teachers that I knew had praised the program because it increased their students' reading and comprehension so much. I wondered, "am I doing something wrong? This program is supposed to be an effective program to increase their reading skills." I kept asking myself questions on what I needed to do to change.

The next thing that came to my mind literally changed the way I taught in the classroom. I was missing the creativity component when teaching the story. There are a lot of our students, especially those who are in urban districts, that lack any kind of internal motivation to do well. They are also looking for the purpose of learning the subject matter that is being taught to them. The scripted program did really what it advertised for a short period of time because it did motivate my students in the short term externally. Part of being a teacher is to motivate our students by teaching them how to motivate themselves. If students do not know how to do this on their own, then we need to find ways in the classroom to teach them how to do it. I came up with the idea of teaching Shakespeare's "Romeo and Juliet" by finding a publication on their reading level and inviting students in from our drama department to act out different scenes of the play. My students would watch how each scene was acted and then discussed with me and their peers what the actors were feeling while they were acting out the different scenes. I then set up discussion groups where the students would discuss with each other the comprehension questions that went with each scene and why the characters were acting the way they were.

What a difference this approach made to my students who not only could they see the words in the book, but also they had a visual in front of them to reinforce the meaning! We discovered together a different way to teach reading and comprehension that was more effective and creative. Not only did the students understand the words that Shakespeare utilized, but they also understood why he used them in his play. We then viewed the Leonardo De Caprio movie version of "Romeo and Juliet" which put a more modern perspective on the play. What I found out was that not only did the students understand what was going on in the film, but they also predicted how the characters were going to act in scenes that were not acted out yet in the movie.

What does this tell us as educators? Scripted programs can be effective to teach students how to read and comprehend stories on a short-term basis, but it is the teacher who supplements the lessons to make learning and offer long-lasting comprehension. From this point on in my career, I used scripted programs as my background for my lessons because I believed in their scientific effectiveness, but I did not believe in their effectiveness for creating an atmosphere of learning in the classroom. That was my job, and I had to make it work for the students who were sitting in front of me.

My name is Jeffrey Dutt, and I am an urban high school history teacher at Louis E. Dieruff High School in Allentown, PA. Throughout my 20 years of teaching, I have learned and adapted my classroom to meet the needs of the students sitting in front of me. Through those experiences along with collaborating with other teaching professionals, I have developed a pathway to become a successful teacher in an often difficult environment to teach.

This book will focus on three main topics, the Educational Landscape, Effective Teaching Techniques, and The Teaching Life. In The Educational Landscape, we will explore the current environment of our modern classrooms. How can a teacher effectively teach in the classroom to have our students become successful? We will also discuss how to develop a classroom that can be effective even in our time of standardized testing. A part of that effectiveness depends on how we can detect issues with students or a classroom as a whole. Teachers who can develop skills in identifying and adjusting academic issues within the classroom before they become problematic will enable students to have a less stressful learning experience. Finally, we will explore how online education has changed the way education is delivered. We will look at the pros and cons of both online and traditional education and their uses for the modern classroom.

In the Effective Teaching Techniques section, we will discuss the characteristics of an effective teacher and how to develop those skills. We will also look at how a teacher can become creative in lesson planning and how to use this when teaching in the classroom. As effective classroom teachers, we need to be able to recognize disruptive behaviors and how to plan and develop techniques to redirect students back to the task at hand. This all leads into the discussion on how a teacher can be seen as an effective leader in the classroom. Effective leadership, developing techniques to change disruptive behaviors, and learning how to be an effective planner leaves nothing to chance for teachers in the classroom.

Finally, we explore the Teaching Life. What inspires teachers to be teachers? We look at what motivates teachers to keep teaching even though they do not see it on a daily basis. We will also discuss the balance that a teacher must maintain between their professional and home lives. This all leads into how teachers can be more prideful in what they do. So many times we see or hear others outside the profession commenting on their thoughts of what teachers do on a daily basis. They knock down our profession and tell us we are overpaid. We will explore how to bring the pride back to our profession and develop ways to open the eyes of those outside the profession.

In this book we would like to inspire you on how new and seasoned teachers can make their professional career less stressful, develop a creative learning environment, and to even help their students raise their scores on standardized tests that we are tasked with every year. We have had the pleasure of interviewing and receiving information from over 25 teachers who teach in an urban, suburban, rural setting from public and private schools to learn from them how to be effective in a classroom. They are current and retired professionals who teach or administrate in early childhood, elementary, middle, and high school level classrooms. Some of the teachers interviewed also teach college classes for students who are learning to become professional teachers. Some of our contributors requested to remain anonymous with their contributions. Their identities have been changed to honor that request. Their contributions to this book are much appreciated.

Part I:
The Landscape

Today's Educational Environment

"A well-educated mind will always have more questions than answers."

— Helen Keller

Education has changed significantly over the last 30 years. Our educational system has developed into a system run by how students score on standardized tests. And yet, the problems that we face in the classroom daily are becoming more complex. We are more focused on finding the correct answer to a question but missing the opportunity to teach our students to find answers on their own. Teachers from many different levels of education and different environments who were interviewed for this book openly discussed issues they face daily. This book focuses on uncovering those issues and offering solutions to those obstacles. Each of these issues will be addressed in specific chapters or throughout the book as they relate to those chapters.

Standardized Testing

Standardized testing is a concern every teacher deals with no matter what subject they teach. We live in a time where test scores provide funding, teacher evaluation scores, achievement for our students, college scholarship money, remediation requirements, and in some cases, graduation rates. Additionally, in some states, a student's advancement into the next grade is contingent on passing scores for the standardized test for the current grade level. These tests are developed by companies or states rather than by classroom teachers. This provides a classroom teacher with a real decision. Should I teach to the test or teach the curriculum? If your job and funding for your school depends on the test scores of a certain group of students, what would you choose?

Unfortunately, many teachers are making the decision to teach to the test to help their students attain a high score. Until just recently in Pennsylvania, (2020), up to 30% of a teacher's evaluation was based on those scores! This poses a problem for a teacher who is evaluated on test scores from different classes. Why? Recently, some states have backed off requirements of teacher evaluation based on student's testing performance. This is a positive measure; using a one-time snapshot to evaluate a teacher's and student's achievement is not an effective tool. It takes all the fun out of education and can cause other problems with which teachers must cope.

In the "Standardized Testing" chapter we will address how a teacher can be effective in the classroom even though there is a strong emphasis on test scores. We will discuss key areas in lesson planning and classroom environment where a teacher can make sure that testing skills along with the curriculum are addressed.

Academic Diagnosticians

In much of the research that was conducted for this book, there is not much data on academic diagnosticians, yet this is what teachers do almost daily in their classrooms. They are expected to observe each of their students to determine if there is a learning problem, such as reading ability or comprehension, writing, calculating, note-taking, test anxiety, or other health concerns as general anxiety, eating issues, or abuse and the list goes on. This is not to say that a teacher should diagnose these issues for a special education diagnosis, but be able to recognize unusual patterns that may flag potential problems for student success..

It is important for a teacher to see if a student is having these problems and to adjust the instruction or curriculum in the classroom to meet the needs of our students since we want all of our students to be able to absorb our lessons in a universal manner. However, unfortunately, that does not happen in the real world, and it certainly does not happen in the classroom. We must make as many modifications to our lessons in order to meet the needs of our students in the classroom.

The chapter titled, "Academic Diagnosticians," will look at how a teacher can spot the learning, physical, and mental issues that can deviate a student from learning effectively in the classroom. We will take a look at some interventions that have helped teachers see these issues and deal with them to keep their students on track.

Characteristics of An Effective Teacher

Not only does a teacher need the training and background to become an excellent teacher, but also needs some qualities to go along with that training. One of the major questions posed to the teachers interviewed was what they considered to be the most important characteristics of an effective teacher. These characteristics can be taught and then applied to enhance classroom lessons and enrich teaching practices.

As previously stated in this chapter, the training that teachers receive throughout the year can help in this area by examining ways to use these characteristics in the classroom. In the "Characteristics of an Effective Teacher" chapter, we discuss what these characteristics are and how a teacher can acquire them. We also look at some classroom situations where these characteristics can be effective and how to use them.

Teacher Training

Many of us who have become teachers received an excellent education in a scientifically based researched curriculum developed for classroom instruction. The curriculum is based on many professional studies that seek to provide our students with background knowledge and finely tuned ways to teach the content. Yet, as mentioned earlier, it also takes the creativity out of teaching if we only follow the program as written in the book. Our students get bored and so do we, especially new teachers, who have really not learned the art of teaching the curriculum.

If we know that this is an issue, then our training during our in-service days should be focused on ways for our teachers to become more effective in this area. We should be allowed to collaborate with each other in our subject areas to discuss effective classroom teaching methods instead of the usual in-service topics often a recycled PowerPoint presentation from previous years that we can all read or by providing us with a binder full of information that we probably will never read. It is very interesting that teachers can repeat word for word every year what is going to be said or taught during these training sessions. The protocol seems for administration to announce "updated" or new mandates that we need to follow, and then, to have us collaborate to see how that works in our classrooms. Teachers need each other to develop teaching techniques to be more effective in the classroom on a daily basis.

If our school or district is insistent on providing these types of in-services year after year then we as teachers need to do more reading on how to be creative. We need to attend more conferences either in person or online that help us become better at what we do. We need to provide ourselves with a learning community where we can share what we learned and let our fellow teachers develop ways of using that information. How much more positive and effective we could be with this proactive format!

Teacher Support

Without a doubt, we as teachers need support. Many other professions such as the medical field provide many years of support after medical school. There is someone always there to help you face a difficult situation, with a course of treatment, or a question that you cannot answer. The same goes for teaching as well. Many teachers complain that once they start teaching in the classroom, they are isolated on their own island. It is totally frustrating and deflating to one's self-esteem when problems arise, and we simply lack the time to collaborate with other teachers or administration. One of the main reasons of low teacher retention rates is because of their seclusion from their colleagues and friendly advice.

We are charged with not only the responsibility to teach the curriculum to our students and enable them to perform effectively on standardized assessments, but also, grade our student's work, related paperwork, lesson planning, communicating with parents and administration, our daily duties, and attending meetings just mention few of our daily responsibilities. We have to find time to effectively do all of this in a timely manner because we cannot afford to fall behind, and because we know we will be evaluated in all of these areas of our professional duties. In the "Balance" chapter, we will discuss time management techniques to develop ways to increase our efficiency. This can assist us in developing stress-relieving techniques to help us focus on areas of improvement.

It bears repeating: we need time to collaborate with each other. A teacher might have a good idea in classroom management or teaching technique that we can adapt to classrooms across the curriculum. Our time is precious and important and we take our job seriously. If we prioritize our time our classroom can become a motivating, enjoyable place to learn for student and teacher.

Is Teacher Burn-Out Real?

In a short answer, yes, teacher burn-out is real. Psychology Today describes teacher burn-out as "a state of chronic stress that leads to physical and emotional exhaustion, cynicism, detachment, feelings of ineffectiveness and lack of accomplishment." This is totally different from feeling tired or overwhelmed. This is when a teacher is not able to mentally and physically recharge or develop effective coping skills. Some of the signs of this burn-out include chronic fatigue, repeated periods of forgetfulness, appetite and weight issues, depression, and anxiety. This causes teachers, who could normally enjoy teaching, to leave the profession early. Studies show that in 2015 there were more than a million teachers who left the teaching profession for most of the reasons listed.

This is an obvious area that needs to be addressed; the issue of recruiting qualified teachers is escalating. Additionally, it has become equally difficult to find and hire qualified substitute teachers to be in the classroom when the regular teacher is absent. We address this problem in the chapter entitled, "The Balance." How do teachers learn to manage their time and stress? We also look at how a teacher can separate their personal lives from their professional lives effectively.

Management of Student Behavior

Every piece of research, conversations with other professional teachers, as well as parents and guardians, and people in the general public eventually seem to turn the conversation to classroom behavior. It is inevitable that a teacher will be faced with some kind of disruptive behavior in their classroom. There are several root causes including, but not limited to, teaching effectiveness, mood of the classroom, mood of the students, lack of an adequate student diet, student conflict, anxiety, attention issues, etc. In the recent COVID-19 pandemic, conversations with parents and friends who have children revealed a renewed interest in their child's teacher and a deepened appreciation for our role. Many reports have shown how ineffective online learning has been in teaching their children and how much valued an effective teacher helps students learn in a classroom.

Why is this such an issue in our profession? It is interesting to me that most college programs who train teachers do not have a specific class or set of procedures to provide for their students. This puts budding teachers at a substantial disadvantage, especially in the urban teaching environment, when faced with behavioral issues and are unable and untrained to effectively respond to the situation. Although we have seen an increase in the number of hours a student from college must spend in observations in the classroom, they still are not equipped with the tools to deal with the behaviors shown by our students. If this does not change, then it is the mentor teacher's responsibility to teach the student teacher how to effectively deal with the disruptive behaviors. Yet, even the mentors do not have the time to help our young teachers to learn these techniques. We need to develop ways to effectively deal with these issues. In the "Dealing with Disruptive Behavior" chapter we will address easy to use techniques that can be used across different classrooms to deal with the disruptions of an everyday classroom.

Communication

One of the areas that continues to frustrate teachers on a daily basis is the lack of communication between the teacher and student, teacher and parent or guardian, teacher and administration, and teacher and the general public. It can be a very frustrating scenario when there is miscommunication between everyone involved in the students' life. It causes more time to be spent in meetings to alleviate problems caused by miscommunication. One of the frustrations I hear regularly from fellow teachers is, "I wish they would listen to us!" We are living in a fast-paced life where everyone wants instantaneous answers to their questions or issues that their child is facing in the classroom. As teachers, we must provide preemptive communication in the beginning of the year to help with open communication. We will discuss this more in the upcoming chapter called, "Effective Communication."

Teachers need to be effective communicators because there is more to teaching than just the curriculum. We will look at how the "hidden curriculum" in the classroom provides our students with ways to think through issues and effective ways to deal with challenges that they face on a daily basis while referring back to the curriculum being taught.

Teachers Seen as Leaders

An effective teacher is seen as a community leader. Most of the teachers that teach in a particular school either live in the community where they teach or live in a community similar to the one they teach in. Because students look up to us for all kinds of different concerns in and out of school, we fulfill a role in the community that cannot be replaced. One of my friends, Tom, has always told me that teachers have, "the second most important job," and, we are vital in not only providing an education but also a base of morals and self-control that a student can use outside of school.

Many of us are also leaders in the community. In 2015 I had the honor of representing my hometown on the Board of Commissioners in the community where I grew up. Other teachers coach a sport, volunteer their time by running an activity or club at school, volunteer with their local church, or volunteer to help others in their neighborhoods. We have to be good stewards of the position in the community in order for us to have pride and to have our community have pride in what we do. This will be addressed in several different chapters as to how much teachers are looked to and the influence that they have.

Online versus Traditional Education

The invention and expansion of the world wide web in the 1990s started a revolution in education called distance learning. It offered an opportunity for students to use the internet to learn outside the traditional classroom. In 1989, Phoenix University launched CompuServe as the first online option for its students. Through many advancements in technology over the past 30 years, online education is now a mainstream option for students and families to consider. During our current Caronavirus pandemic, online education has become more of a necessity. Most traditional education outlets had to convert to online education for the safety and well-being of the teachers, students, and the public.

Will this become more of an option once there is an advancement of a vaccine or will in-person education continue to be a major part of the landscape? We need to take a look at the advantages and disadvantages of online education as a platform to teach our kids in the future.

There are many positive reasons to be proud about being a teacher which are included in some inspirational stories in this book. Sometimes we lose sight of the honor and dignity we have as teachers. We need to be reminded that we make a difference and that is what this book is about. We need to take back who we are and what we do. It is a very difficult job, but if we continue to learn and change with what is needed we will thrive as a profession. The following chapters attempt to provide you with ways to make your classroom run more smoothly and to make your life easier.

Standardized Testing

"If my future were just determined by my performance on standardized tests, I wouldn't be here. I guarantee you that."

— Former First Lady Michelle Obama

History of Standardized Testing

One form or another of standardized testing has been around in our country and the rest of the world for over 150 years. According to the National Educational Association timeline, the first oral standardized tests were given to students before 1840. After this, students were given written tests because the focus of education was not to just educate the elite but to educate the masses.

The early forms of standardized testing were used to show students with a lot of promise in higher education such as college. This would separate them from those who would need more resources to reach their potential. In and around 1920, this test used to show academic promise was renamed the Scholastic Aptitude Test or SAT.

In the 1960s there was a surge in standardized testing because of the appearance of a globalized economy. These tests also helped show if the students in the United States were being prepared to become part of a skilled workforce. It attempted to bring a spotlight on the learning in the classroom and tie it to the scores on the achievement tests. The reason these were used by colleges was because it brought the availability of college to the masses and not just the elite.

The No Child Left Behind Act of 2001 was a much-touted piece of legislation by the federal government. This changed the way teachers taught in class by changing the curriculum in order for students to achieve Yearly Adequate Progress in both reading and mathematics. It also changed the way teachers were certified, and it made receiving a certificate more difficult under those standards. If students in the school did not make adequate progress on these tests, there would be an increasing number of sanctions on the school to improve their scores including the threat of closure if the school continued to underperform. The goal here was to improve the scores of minority students over time to increase to make a more level playing field as compared to non-minority students.

In 2015, the Obama Administration introduced the Every Student Succeeds Act (ESSA). This legislation changed the federal government's role in how and when a state would administer standardized testing. It provided states with more latitude on how it would deal with schools that were underperforming on these tests. It also eliminated the "highly qualified" requirement for teachers in core subjects. Finally, it gave states the permission to develop their own teacher evaluation system without federal input.

So, as you can see, standardized testing has changed over time from when it started. It is a way for states to evaluate how students are doing or does it? We will explore the pros and cons of standardized testing in the next section.

Pros and Cons of Standardized Testing

There are some pros to having a way to evaluate student's achievement by using standardized tests. The use of standardized testing can provide parents and students ways to compare them to other students their same age. This is called Norm-Referenced Testing. It compares the achievement of a student against other students of the same age, school, district, city, county and country. It provides data to show how they are performing in the same core subjects as their peers. In the same comparison, it can provide problem areas that a student is experiencing so that a teacher can provide extra help in those areas of learning. If used within the school year, it could be used as a starting point or strategy to help a student achieve at a higher level within that subject.

Another pro or advantage to utilizing standardized testing is that it provides a structure for a teacher to teach a curriculum. The teacher has a pretty good idea of the information that the students will be tested. It also provides a structure for the state or the country to be teaching the same type of materials in the subject being taught. This then goes with the testing because then everyone can be tested on the same information being taught in all of the same classrooms.

One more advantage of standardized testing is that it eliminates bias in grading procedures. If every student no matter where they go to school is tested on the same information then it eliminates any bias in grading. Therefore, there will be no subjective grading by the teacher because there is only one way to grade the answers because all of the curriculum across the state or country would be the same.

The last advantage to standardized testing is that the test can show what a particular student or classroom has difficulty with in the areas of math, reading, or writing. The information can be used to either re-teach or enhance the learning in the classroom where students are struggling. It actually does pinpoint where students struggle and helps develop specific lessons to help students in that specific area.

However, there are some real downfalls or cons to standardized testing. A one-time test does not really show what a student has learned over the past year. There is too much emphasis on each student achieving well on a one-time test that is designed to show progress over a year's time. If a student does not score well on a particular test, the student will feel more pressure in that particular subject thereby lowering their confidence and ability. Let's face it, not all of us are good in every subject nor are we good test-takers. If we continually score low in a particular subject area, we will want to avoid it as much as possible. It can also provide a student with negative feelings toward that subject and want to make them not attend that particular class even if it is required for their graduation to the next grade or from high school.

Another con to standardized testing is teachers have a tendency to teach to the test rather than teaching the curriculum in a subject area. This provides the classroom with more information and less creativity. We will look at creativity in the classroom later in Chapter 4. This also can produce boredom in the students and the classroom because there is no focus on teaching cognitive skills and which hampers students' learning potential in the classroom.

A third con is that standardized testing does not consider any external factors that can affect a student's performance on the test. Since the tests are a one-time snapshot of a student's proficiency they do not take into consideration factors that can affect a student's performance such as the student's home-life. Problems at home definitely carry over to the classroom and can affect a student's mindset. Also, it does not take into account if a student is tired, hungry, or a lower performing test-taker.

A fourth con for standardized testing is that it does not consider other aspects of learning that the student may show. For instance, standardized tests do not take that into consideration student creativity into consideration as there is only one answer per question. Unmotivated students who feel the test means nothing will underperform.

Finally, a major con is that the people who design the standardized tests think differently than teachers. They only look at the questions themselves. They do not take into consideration the way a student with a different language who is learning English for the first time would read the question. Nor do they take into consideration the needs of special education students who may not read on the level that the question is being asked or understand the vocabulary used in the question. Most of the time, teachers are unable to help students with these issues during the test. This increases frustration and the feeling of inadequacy of the student, and they have a tendency to give up on the test without trying.

Are We Using Standardized Testing for the Right Reasons?

This is a major question that we face as teachers on a daily basis. There is so much emphasis on achievement on these tests and without enough focus on areas that students need like life-long learning and critical thinking. Somehow, we have made college the achievement that every student should attain yet, standardized tests are not used to see if a student can graduate from high school nor show if they would be successful in college. Is this the ultimate focus and cumulative purpose of a student's education?

Somehow going to college has become the pinnacle of a student's career and that misses the mark for real life skills. Take it from this college graduate who does not know how to stop a leak, fix an electrical problem, or hang drywall. If instruction could link curriculum with student aptitudes – where personal inclinations and experiences relate directly to their success – and real life applications, we would be setting up our students for success. Rather, we are doing this when we are setting them up for failure by requiring our students to achieve high scores on standardized tests.

Students are not one size fits all learners. Some students are particularly good at math, science, reading, writing, social studies, or even the fine arts. There are some students who might be good at all of these subjects, but not everyone is. If a student is not proficient in one of those academic areas but is still expected to score well on a one-time test, we have missed the mark with the wrong approach for testing. It is supposed to provide a teacher with a tool to help struggling students in a certain subject area – to provide remediation and to develop the skills that are needed to pass a standardized test. If we cannot use the tests for that purpose, they lose their effectiveness.

For example, in a college class that I was teaching recently at Lehigh Carbon Community College a student raised her hand to ask a question when we were discussing standardized testing. Mary was a paraprofessional in a local school district learning to become a certified teacher. She overheard the principal of the school giving a tour to a new teacher who was hired for the upcoming school year. As the principal was walking the hallway with a new hire pointing out who teaches in different classrooms, the principal would state the teacher's name, grade, and achievement level of his or her students on the previous year's standardized test. For instance, she would say, "This is Mrs. Haber's room; she teaches 3rd grade, and her students scored 98% proficiency on the PSSA last year! This is Ms. Thames' classroom; she also teaches 3rd grade." The principal did not say anything about the achievement of Ms. Thames' students because they did not achieve a high mark on the standardized test. Should this be a reflection on the teacher? We know nothing about Ms. Thames's students; perhaps many of her students had Individualized Education Plans (IEP), were they English Language Learners (ELA), had other factors like mental illness, hunger, physical, emotional, or mental issues that affected how they did on the test that day? No, student scores should not be a reflection on the teacher, but we as a country have put an inordinate emphasis on these tests, and our politicians base our school's funding on those test scores.

Samantha, an elementary school Kindergarten teacher in a suburban school district in Pennsylvania, told me that she is required to teach word for word from the curriculum to make sure that her students do well on the standardized testing that they will be required to take in the future. We cannot predict how a student will do based on a scripted program provided in the classroom. In fact, we will be limiting the learning potential of our students because their achievement will be based on responses rather than how they were able to arrive to the correct answer. She also shared this policy limits the teacher's ability to see students who are experiencing learning problems because it does not require them to read. It only requires that students respond correctly in a chorus.

There is Hope with The Age of Standardized Testing

Having outlined the pros and cons of standardized testing and shown that we are utilizing the tests in the incorrect manner, there are ways we can bring back some effective teaching techniques to enable high student achievement both in the classroom and on the standardized tests.

We can bring back the fun into teaching as you will see in the following chapters as we discuss how a professional teacher can look at issues in the classroom from an individual basis or an entire classroom to change the environment for the better. We can become academic diagnosticians.

There are two concepts that are forgotten by teachers as they enter the classroom because we are pressured to have students do well on these tests. So, in the next section of our journey of being an effective teacher, we will look at characteristics of a professional who is effective in the classroom in chapter 5, and in chapter 6, we will discover that we can have a creative classroom in the age of standardized testing.

Today, one of the areas that a teacher needs to become more skilled in the classroom is dealing with disruptive behaviors effectively. In chapter 7, "Dealing with Disruptive Behaviors," we will look at how we can deal with these unsettling behaviors because if they are not dealt with early and succinctly, all of our students will be affected – both in the classroom and on the tests.

Teachers are like the captain of a ship. We lead the classroom and provide it with direction. In Chapter 8, "Teachers as Leaders," we will look at how a teacher can become an effective leader and to show students ways to achieve on a daily basis to combat the cons of testing as stated above.

Teachers need to also think of how to plan their lessons in order for students to gain as much knowledge as possible. In Chapter 9, "Don't Leave Anything to Chance," we will discuss how a teacher effectively lesson plans as they reflect on the different aspects of each lesson from what we want our students to know at the end of every step to get to that point. We need to be ready for any unexpected situations in the classroom to arise so that we do not lose the momentum already underway in the classroom.

From here on, we will learn to become a better profession by drawing from the knowledge, experiences, wisdom, and advice of qualified teachers within our profession.

Academic Diagnosticians

"We must not, in trying to think about how much we can make a difference, ignore the small daily differences we can make which, over time add up to the big differences we cannot foresee."

— Marian Wright Edelman

Overview

The Merriam-Webster Dictionary defines a diagnostician as "serving to distinguish or identify." A teacher is a person who looks at individual students, a classroom, and a learning community every day and sees aspects of each of these that are working really well. We should also have the ability to develop skills that pinpoint areas that are not working well, but developing those skills is a difficult task because it is something that is developed over time, often through trial and error. However, if we can identify and acquire these skills early in our career, with continued application and practice we can fine tune them. We will be focusing on these skills in the three key areas listed above and how to effectively use them.

Individual Students

Students with disruptive behaviors (see chapter 7) bring their own unique skill sets and environments with them when they enter our classroom. Each individual student will exhibit skills that indicate their uniquely giftedness or deficiencies. Once we identify those gifts and deficits we must base our lesson plans and tailor instruction based on those variances. An individual student may struggle with attention span issues, a history of failing classes with lack of motivation, lack of focus, reading difficulties, difficulty with computation skills, or a history of disruptive behaviors. Any of these can make a teacher's experience in the classroom a challenging one and dilute our effectiveness by primarily focusing on the issues. How can we spot these issues before they become a problem and then develop a solution to refocus the classroom climate?

There are signs and symptoms that we as teachers need to look for in order to help define what is going on with individual students. One of the first signs that a student signals that there is a problem is boredom. This may be a sign of a student either not understanding the content or that the content is too easy for him. Putting their pen or pencil or even a head down on the desk, not listening to the instructions, or doing something else in the classroom that catches their attention is like a person listening to a radio talk show in an unrecognizable language or when the host is talking to the audience about a subject as though they were an infant. The solution? Privately speak to the student to get their perspective and either adjust their curriculum, alter instruction, or provide individual instruction depending on when we provide independent work in our classroom. Also, make sure to contact the parents or guardians to keep them appraised of what we observe and are planning to do to make the situation better. Often, a conversation with them will shed more light on the student, especially if you ask if they see similar behavior at home.

Another sign to look for is lack of motivation. Perhaps the student in our class has a history of low grades, and the teacher realizes that they are not doing any of the assigned classwork or homework. This may be an indication that the student is not motivated to do work in our class. Certainly, this is an issue every teacher faces, but left unchecked it will provide undue frustration and stress.

Solution? Develop a strategy for this student that will provide external or extrinsic motivators and then transform them into intrinsic motivators. We can provide individual motivators to our students to try and increase motivation. For example, if a student has had a history of low performance, it might be because they are not used to being successful and low performance has become a habit. We might question ourselves if the student is a deep, strategic, or surface thinker. Surface thinkers are students who just want to avoid failing. A strategic thinker is a student who is only motivated by their grades. A deep thinker is a student who likes the challenge of a difficult concept and figuring out the complexities of the task. They are very intrinsically motivated. Identify the type of thinker the student is then develop tasks that will intrinsically motivate them. One of my former students responded well to this strategy.

Brian was struggling academically in the 9th grade. His parents were frustrated because they did not know what was going on to cause their son to struggle academically and were considering a special education service evaluation. Up until high school, his academic performance was not the greatest, but it was good enough for him to move on to the next grade. When we met, Brian was not completing his assignments, was disorganized, and stated he was not motivated to complete any of his assignments. His test grades were suffering, and there was a concern that he would have to attend summer school.

During a home visit, I was talking with Brian after his parents briefed me on their concerns. He was very articulate and intelligent, but revealed to me how unmotivated he was and how much pressure he felt that everyone was putting on top of him to do well in school. After we spoke for a while, I asked him to show me what he was doing in his classes and the homework that he was asked to complete. I quickly realized that Brian was a surface learner and just wanted to get by to pass his classes, and at the time, did not require special education services. I reassured his parents that I would keep them appraised if Brian did not respond to our new action plan and reconsider special education services. We set up a place for him to do his work, organized his notebooks, and I taught him how to increase his self-awareness in learning. One of the ways we did this was to "chunk" his work into small pieces. Once he accomplished small goals, we then lengthened the chunk of work until he was completing work on his own. Using this technique, Brian gradually started completing more and more school work, and his grades continued to improve. I am very proud to say that Brian just made Dean's List at our local community college, and he keeps me posted on his progress toward a teaching degree in social studies.

Another red flag that a student needs assistance is when a student is spending a lot of time completing classwork or homework. This is a sign that the student is struggling with the content, whether it is reading, answering the questions (comprehension), or being constantly distracted by others in the classroom or at home. The student also may not ask questions during the instruction because they do not want to feel "dumb" compared to their peers. When this happens, we need to start asking the student questions and then develop a plan, such as providing extra time to complete assignments. The goal is to help the student not become overwhelmed with classwork but still be able to grasp the concepts needed in each lesson.

A student who is not getting enough sleep or not eating properly is another indicator that contributes to disruptive behavior. Many students come from environments where they do not get enough proper sleep or eat a proper diet; others do not have a regular routine to follow. They eat when they can and sleep when they can. Imagine us teaching without getting much sleep or being able to drink our coffee in the morning. We could not be possibly ready or willing to be the best that we are capable of being while we are facing a classroom of active students. It is vital that schools provide students with breakfast and lunch every day to help them be ready to learn in the classroom. We should also encourage our students to go to bed and wake up every day at regular times. Our students, no matter what age, need to have a daily routine to follow in order to do and be at their best. Otherwise, they spend each day without the energy or effort needed to succeed in the classroom.

Finally, a change in behaviors is a tell-tale sign that a student is struggling academically. Students rarely speak up about their academic struggles, but instead, develop avoidance behaviors, such as refusing to do work, refusing to speak about their assignments, distracting other students, exhibiting increased frustration with assignments, and expectations put on them. This can be not only for the student, but for the teacher as well. When there is a sudden change in behavior, there is a problem! We need to discreetly and privately chat with the student to discover what has changed and develop an individual plan with the student to reverse the pattern. This is an important step because it telegraphs our true concern for the student as well as provides a listening ear when it is needed.

Now that we looked at the signs and symptoms of a struggling student we can focus on the classroom environment.

The Classroom Environment

Yes, there are those classes that challenge us the most those that push our buttons. It can be the personalities that are in the classroom, the level of ability of the student, our didactic method, classroom structure, or other variables. The ability of a teacher to recognize that they need to change and develop a different strategy to deal with this problematic class is key to increasing success and lowering frustration for student and teacher alike. It is said that the definition of insanity is if you always do what you've always done, you'll always get what you got. To that end, we will talk about a few specific instances.

Students bring diverse abilities to our classroom. Some classes may be easy to teach because the students are intrinsically motivated, have no questions, and complete their work in a timely manner. Then there is the class or two that listens very well, struggles with the material, but with some assistance can complete the work with some extra time. Then there are those classes that struggle to pay attention, are not motivated to complete the work, and increase our stress level because we struggle with adapting to meet their needs. What do you do with these kinds of classes?

While routine is a critical component to have in the classroom, however, not every class will be able to perform with that routine. A teacher must have the ability to modify the way they are teaching to the classroom dynamics. For example, more direct instruction and less independent work would be a more appropriate approach for a class that requires that modification even though the teacher has always expected the students to complete assignments independently with less instruction. We need to also change our grading system when it comes to each individual class. This needs to be recognized quickly by the teacher because it will provide them with a routine for every class.

For example, I was in a new school in my 14th year of teaching. I had a mix of 9th grade and 11th grade history classes. Most of my classes were very good and easily adapted to the class routine. However, one 9th grade class needed most of my help to get through the class, all 34 of them! On top of that, history was the last class of the day, and all they wanted to do was leave school. They were not motivated to do any assignments and tried to avoid as much work as possible. I had a difficult time transitioning from my motivated classes to my unmotivated class. I decided, too late by my own standards looking back, to do more direct instruction/project based curriculum lessons to calm the storm of apathy I faced at the end of the day. Because they had to meet a certain number of milestones within the class period in order to achieve their class goal, they began to get their work done. I learned a valuable lesson;

I needed to look at the culture of each class and develop strategies to effectively teach who was in front of me.

A key to confident, effective teaching is to recognize our classroom needs to change to meet the needs of the individuals who are looking at us. This class culture is something that needs to be positive for the students, or you will lose them one by one. Students are very good at picking up the mood in a classroom and will adjust to what is being shown by other students and their teacher. In the above example, the student's radars were reading my frustration loud and clear and used that to their advantage at least until I was able to catch on that something needed to change. The quicker we get wise to the class climate, the greater likelihood of a wiser class.

The School as a Community

The school culture is another area that needs to be diagnosed and changed as needed. It is important that the students, faculty, and administration are on the same page when it comes to developing a culture. It is something that needs to be consistently implemented across the board and everyone understands and knows what to expect on a daily basis. We should be able to look to our experienced teachers within the building to develop that culture. What should a school culture look like? Two teachers I spoke with provided me with insights into this issue: Mr. Dale Weiss, social studies teacher and department chair, at an inner-city high school in Allentown, PA for the past 30+ years, and Mrs. Peg Shaw, English teacher and department chair at the same high school for 30+ years in Allentown, PA.

The main message they both shared with me is to make sure that the school is a true community. If a teacher is seeing that a student is struggling, this should be communicated to other teachers, the administration, and the family. Too often, the signs and symptoms of an academic problem can be hidden effectively by the student, but it can be shown in multiple classes. Therefore, this needs to be a team approach. We must find out if the academic issue that is evident in our classroom might also be apparent in other classrooms or other settings. If that is the case, then we can take a team approach to assess it, take notes, and figure out a way to effectively deal with it across the board. The consistency and concern of the entire team go a long way to help a student be successful.

However, if we find the issue is isolated and happening in only our classroom, we must look in the mirror and figure out why the way we are instructing the student is not effective. As suggested by Dale and Peg, we should ask others for help. One of the most difficult things that a teacher experiences, especially someone that is new, is to admit that we need help. It is a very isolating experience if we do not align ourselves with others who can help us be successful in the classroom. To become someone that we want to be in the classroom, we must watch and talk to others who are effective and emulate that in our classroom.

Both of these experienced teachers also shared that there needs to be a consistent way of dealing with problems across the school building itself. For example, if there is an agreed-upon procedure about student expectations and behavior toward classmates and teachers in the hallway or classroom, then that policy needs to be consistently followed by every staff member. If there is shown to be a consistent problem with an individual student or group of students in these settings, then the administration and the parents need to be brought into the situation. A team approach to these problems not only shows consistency within the school, but provides a teacher with the feeling of community support as opposed to dealing with an issue on an island by themselves. Providing this kind of consistency shows the students, faculty, public, and administration how effective a community can learn and act.

Unfortunately, this is not always the case in our schools. We need to be more consistent with how we develop school-wide plans and not change them from year to year depending on what is the new and greatest programs that are developed in our profession. If a program for our school is not producing what we would like it to, then together, we need to look at what is not working and change that before moving on to a new program that would provide our school or district with more expense and training. This shows the faculty, the students, and the families that we are using the program to develop a learning community dedicated to helping students become the best that they can be. Without this team approach, frustration and discontent is fostered in the students and faculty.

There is a rather new way in the delivery of education, online. In the next chapter, we will discuss the pros and cons of both online and traditional education delivery systems. Can both of these systems exist separately? In a word, yes. But, are they as effective separately or working together? We will explore and answer this question in the next chapter.

Online Versus Traditional Education

"Teachers need to integrate technology seamlessly into the curriculum instead of using it as an add-on, an afterthought, or an event."

— Heidi Hayes Jacobs, Owner, Curriculum Designers, Inc.

Introduction

As stated earlier, online education has been around since 1989. In reading an article by Hope E. Kentnor entitled, "Curriculum and Teaching Dialogue," from 2015, the author states, "Online education is no longer a trend. Rather, it is mainstream." It is pretty clear that online education is here to stay as part of the education landscape. It is true that we live in a digital world. Most of the students from elementary school through college, own or have access to a cell phone, computer, or tablet. Now that we are dealing with the Coronavirus and the discontinuation of in-person instruction, online instruction has come to the forefront of the delivery of education. We need to discuss how much of the instruction provided for today's youth should be conducted in an online platform. We will discuss the pros and cons of each educational delivery system, how technology can be integrated into the traditional classroom, and where education will be trending in the future.

Pros and Cons of Online Instruction

Online learning has definitely changed the way education is taught. The introduction of such programs as Moodle, Blackboard, Edgenuity, Eztalk, Loom, Zoom, Google Classroom, and others has really changed the landscape. The inclusion of these programs brings up some interesting questions. Should our current and new teachers learn how to teach online? Will traditional education be replaced by online learning? To answer these questions, let us first discuss the pros and cons of this form of education and how it changes the way education is delivered.

One of the first pros of online education is the flexibility in scheduling. Students can log in to the platform used by the school and can complete their assignments 24 hours a day. Students, under the supervision of their parents, can log in and complete assignments, quizzes, and tests when it is most convenient for them. There are times when a student needs to be on the program to be taught by a teacher live, but then they have the flexibility to complete their assignments when it is convenient to their schedule. There continues to be a deadline for the student to complete assignments, but they do not have to hand in a paper version to the teacher. Their assignments can be delivered to the teacher via email or on the actual platform. Google Classroom, as an example, provides students and teachers an easy way for developing a dialogue for questions or comments, and to hand in assignments. The teacher is able to provide comments and grades for each of these assignments. The program keeps a running grade-book for the teacher to grade assignments, and for the student and parents to view their grades in real time.

Another advantage to an online educational platform is that it is very student-centered. Students are able to respond to the course material and to other student posts. Students respond to other posts that clearly speak to their individual concerns. Basically, they speak to students in a smaller forum rather than a larger classroom. Students control their own learning which is geared towards their own individual needs. Those students who are traditionally introverted can respond more easily to prompts and assignments without worrying about how and when they respond.

A third advantage of online learning is its convenience. There is no need to transport students back and forth to a building to learn. The internet provides ample access to information from around the world in order to complete their assignments. There are no costs for textbooks, or the storage of them, because students have access to an unlimited amount of information from the internet. You can also learn from a comfortable place, your home. You can dress in your favorite comfortable outfits to go to school. There is no need to show your best looks because you are learning at home. Imagine how much time you would save by not driving back and forth to a physical building, battling traffic, or the time you would spend purchasing your favorite beverage at a local convenience store on your way to that building.

A final advantage of online learning is synergy. Each student has the opportunity to respond to the teacher and other students in the class. Many ideas and resources are shared between instructors and students. Students are less afraid to share these ideas with the teacher without the anxiety of interrupting a lecture or other students contributing in class. The fear of retribution from other students is lessened, which provides an atmosphere of sharing these ideas.

While online education provides several advantages to educating our students, there are some definite cons to this platform as well. One of the disadvantages that is discussed quite a bit when it comes to online education, is socialization. Human beings are very social creatures. We learn so much by interacting with others. Whether it is verbal or non-verbal cues, it is more difficult to communicate with others in an online portal. Students in a traditional educational setting are often encouraged to complete group work or to discuss concepts learned in class with their peers. They participate in after-school activities including sports and clubs, where they learn how to socialize with other students from different socioeconomic and cultural backgrounds. This only enhances how we interact with each other.

A second disadvantage that is common to online learning is a student who learns online needs to be self-motivated. If you are not a self-motivated or disciplined type of person, online education will be very diffi-cult. Many students, especially in the inner-city schools, lack the moti-vation or discipline to be successful in an online experience. I have seen many students return to traditional schools because of the lack of self-motivation to keep up with the curriculum in an online setting. A more traditional educational setting can help students who lack this very im-portant trait to build that self-motivation by developing a relationship with the teacher and other adults in the school who can help teach a student to become more self-motivated.

A third disadvantage of online education is the availability and vari-ety of programming available to students. Although opportunities for a variety of programs have increased in the online platform, traditional schools continue to have more programs available for students to choose from. An example of programs that would be more difficult to perform online would be science labs, physical education, and other courses that require more hands-on learning. Each state has its own re-quirements for education. A parent has to search programs that meet these requirements in online programs, while traditional schools al-ready match those requirements provided by the state.

Finally, another disadvantage is learning style. The traditional edu-cation model is more geared toward many different learning styles. If you are an auditory or visual learner, online education is perfect for these types of students. These online platforms have not figured out how to cater to kinesthetic or social learners, as of yet. It is important to figure out what type of learner your child is to fit their needs as best as possible.

Pros and Cons to Traditional Educational

Traditional or conventional education provides students many ad-vantages over online education. One of those advantages is that tradi-tional education is very well planned. The programs and the day are very organized when it comes to class times and after-school activities.

Everything is pre-planned for you, whether it is your daily routine, right down to what you can and cannot wear in school. The atmosphere is geared toward providing students and faculty with a regular daily schedule, and they do not have to worry about too many changes. This helps students build structure and self-discipline in respect to being able to follow a certain schedule and adhere to expectations within that schedule.

Another advantage to traditional education is face-to-face interaction. Students can easily solve complex problems through group interactions. They also have physical access to the teacher in the classroom. The teacher is able to provide individual guidance and expertise of their field, in person. This builds an invaluable relationship between teacher and student. Bonds are formed that are much more difficult to form in an online format.

Third, traditional education provides hands-on training. For subjects like biology, chemistry, physics, psychology, sociology, and others, the traditional system provides avenues for students to experiment with concepts that they are learning in class. It taps into the kinesthetic and other learning styles that online education would have a difficult time providing. Also, students can use what they learn in their classes, while participating in extracurricular activities and clubs during and after school. It is also an opportunity for students to see their teachers in different roles outside the classroom. Students can see and experience their teachers in roles of leadership other than teaching.

Finally, traditional education provides students with a sense of competition. Our world is a very competitive place. We need students to be able to compete not only with students in their own school, but also with students from across the state, country, and world. This provides a sense of motivation to be better than the next person. It teaches students how to internally motivate themselves to be the best that they can be, and then transfers this motivation to a college or work setting. When students learn this, they are able to compete for recognition, which provides a higher value of education than when the competitiveness is removed.

Traditional education also has its disadvantages. The cost of traditional education is expensive. The expense is paid through tax programs, county and state taxes, tuition, and loans. At times of financial distress, like we are currently dealing with in our country, budgets can become tight to pay for facilities, extra-curricular activities, and cafeteria services. In these times, services provided by the school may be curtailed or eliminated altogether. This is where politics enter the equation, which can make the financial picture more stressful. Depending on how the local, state, or federal budget is, determines how much funding a school will receive. It seems that this has become a yearly struggle between citizens and the government. This struggle will continue as long as budgets are linked to political discussions.

A second disadvantage of traditional education is students can become passive learners. Our students are not always required to actively participate in what is going on in the classroom. If this takes place, the students' main source of information is the teacher. The students become dependent on the teacher for their information and have a tendency to not research information on their own. This passivity may cause education to become boring and dull, which affects an individual student's motivation to compete and motivate themselves to learn.

Another con of traditional education is the evaluation system that is used to see if students are retaining and using the information taught in the classroom. Most testing in classrooms is based on memorization of facts and digits. Testing is mostly focused on information that you learn during the time you are in that particular classroom. It does not test the accumulated knowledge that students have learned throughout their time as a student. It also doesn't test all of your abilities. It only tests what you know and does not explain what you understand.

Finally, the traditional classroom lacks the ability to teach students to think critically. As we are testing students on their memorization of facts, dates, and digits, it does not teach students how to apply the knowledge they are accumulating. It also has difficulty showing how the knowledge students are learning in class are related. Unfortunately, with the routine that traditional educational setting provides, there is little time for students to learn how to utilize the knowledge in a deep and profound way. If they had time to learn and utilize these skills, they would become better problem solvers with the knowledge they attain.

Solutions for Education

For traditional and online education to be effective for our students, we need to have a blended system. Our educational system should combine the advantages of technology with our traditional education system. This can provide, not only individualized education for our students, but also develop the critical socialization skills needed to be a productive part of society. Here are some suggestions on how to accomplish this.

School Districts and private institutions should offer both online and traditional options. Individual goals would be set for each individual student, and through those sessions, determine which educational model would be best used to reach those goals. A student may be better served with traditional or online education. They may need to have a blended program that offers both for the student. Technology and the availability of internet access should be a top priority if this system is designed correctly. Through a routine evaluation of a student's needs, we can determine which courses would be learned online, in a traditional education setting, or in a blended course.

Another advantage to this system is that students would be monitored more closely by their teachers. With online access to information needed for both types of learning atmospheres, students will have a more difficult time falling behind. Teachers would be able to monitor the progress of their students online and provide helpful tips and encouragement for students who are struggling. It would also provide an opportunity for parents to be more involved in students' education. Parents would be able to see where their sons or daughters are struggling, and teachers and parents would be able to collaborate more to help the students.

A third advantage of a blended education system is that our students become more proficient in their digital skills. Most jobs in the United States and across the world require that applicants be proficient in tech skills. In traditional school settings, we need to have our students learn the programs necessary to compete in the current job market. Some jobs that our students will apply for will pay more if an applicant is proficient in programs such as Microsoft Office and others.

Another advantage to a blended program would be cost control. A bold solution to the funding issues that school districts face, is to provide more online learning to cut costs of the physical buildings and transportation. This would relieve the taxpayer burden on education and funds can be used from those savings to enhance the educational experience for our students. Since our students are technologically more savvy these days, it would make sense to invest in those skills to deliver a better education product.

Now that we looked at the overall landscape of what educators are facing, we need to answer the questions of what teachers need to do to be successful in our schools? What kinds of strategies do we need in order for our students to be successful under our leadership? We will answer these questions in our next section on Effective Teaching.

Part II:
Effective Teaching

Characteristics of Effective Teachers

"A good teacher like, a good entertainer, must first hold his audience's attention, then he can teach his lesson."

— John Henrik Clarke

Overview

Throughout their teaching career, many teachers learn effective ways to teach lessons. Unfortunately, one of the areas a teacher needs to develop outside those lessons are personality characteristics that will make them more effective; these skills are not always easy to develop. In fact, it is entirely possible that we will have to change our teaching philosophy to realize and refine these qualities to grab the attention of our students. But, having these traits will help make our jobs more fulfilling and less stressful. In this chapter, we will share those traits or characteristics and discuss how we develop them and use them in the classroom.

Patience

The first attribute that comes through loud and clear is patience. Developing patience as a teacher is not the easiest characteristic to accomplish and is certainly developed over time. But, if one is not patient how do you develop it? What does patience look like in the classroom?

Overall, our society today does not demonstrate much patience as is evidenced by social media. Stories feature people with the lack of answers, others waiting rudely in line, people who are intolerant of others' opinions, or others unwilling to slow down in a 25 mile per hour speed zone. So, for a teacher in today's hurry-up culture, teaching patience is like teaching a new language. We not only teach it but we also have to live it. There is nothing more intrinsically essential to a relationship with others than to show patience. Building effective relationships with our students, starts with patience. It is rightly said that "the fastest way to get anything done is to slow down." When we are able to slow our minds down, we can think straighter. We are able to answer the same question over and over without becoming frustrated. This also involves excellent classroom planning skills as we discuss this in more depth in Chapter 9, "Don't Leave Anything to Chance." If we leave time during our lesson to calmly and clearly answer student questions, we will not feel rushed as we cram everything in before the period bell rings. So, how do we as teachers help young people develop this characteristic?

First, it is invaluable to be involved or observe where the teacher is not only patient in response to the students but also models patience to them. Many of the teachers that I have observed over the years were very good at being patient with their students; when they asked a question of their students, they would actually wait at least 30 seconds for a response. A technique called Silent Seconds which provided the students enough time to think about or look up the answer. The reverse would also be true if a student asked a question of the teacher; the teacher actually listened to the student, thought for a time about how to answer the question, and then responded. If the teacher did not know the answer, they went and found the answer. The whole time these situations unfolded, the teacher was being intentionally patient and teaching patience.

Another technique to teach this elusive quality, especially with younger students is by placing circles or shapes on the classroom floor leading to the door and out into the hallway. If the student is completing the activity too quickly, the adult has the student count on each spot before moving on; then there is a transition to another activity outside the classroom. It looks like this: a student will put their belongings or supplies away. They will then go over to the first circle, and they will count to a certain number. Once they are finished they move to the next circle and do the same. This provides other students who are cleaning up or are not quite finished with their task to catch up to line up at the door with their peers who were counting on the shapes. This provides more independence and movement to the students and gives the teacher more opportunity to help other students in the classroom. To make this work effectively the teacher must model the routine several times so that the students understand what they are required to do.

Flexibility

Along with patience, a teacher needs to demonstrate flexibility. This is so evident in our classrooms today. Teachers are bombarded with distractions in the classroom. During the course of the lesson, a student may ask to go to the bathroom, the classroom phone rings throughout the lesson, a behavior problem arises on one side of the room while a student is looking at phone on the other side, an announcement comes over the public address system – the possibilities are endless. We need to be able to allow for these distractions when we plan our lessons to actually build in time to accommodate the unexpected. This essentially circumvents the frustration of not finishing the lesson. I usually place anywhere from 2-5 minutes of distraction time into my lessons; if I anticipate interruptions, my lesson is not derailed.

Another example where a teacher needs to be flexible is in their explanations of complicated topics. There are not many students that are going to understand the subject we are teaching as we do. We need to simplify and vary our explanation. For instance, I was teaching my students how to write a research paper in history class. We had been studying the decade of the 1920s, and we were looking at influential famous people and its outcomes. We were discussing Babe Ruth, Al Capone, Jack Dempsey, Albert Einstein, Al Jolson, and others. The students had to choose someone to research and write a paper describing how their chosen person was influential. The students were not getting the concept that you could not copy and paste information from the internet and nor how to properly cite the source. Students had their own ideas of putting together a research paper based on previous experiences while other students had never even written a research paper. So, I had to be flexible and include easy to understand instructions on how to do the research, cite their information properly, and put it all together.

I decided to use a method that I learned a long time ago when I was in high school. Mrs. Hale, my one English teacher whom I admired, taught us to scaffold everything. Scaffolding is basically building from your knowledge base and learning new information on top of it. I had to figure out where each student was with their knowledge of writing a proper research paper and build from there. It was a lesson component that I had not anticipated, but had to include to reduce their frustration and mine. Remember, there will be classes that need more or less help; we have to be able to anticipate this in each class and plan to modify to accommodate those needs.

Organization Skills

Organizational skills are the critical component of an effective teacher. One of the teachers that I interviewed, June Fritchey, a 12th grade special education teacher at an urban high school in Allentown, PA, stated emphatically that organization is the most important characteristic for a teacher to possess. June juggles several different inclusion classes along with over 20 IEPs to write and monitor throughout the year. She must be organized since most of these IEPs do not involve students that she would see daily, therefore, she must rely on other teachers and their observations to make sure that the goals and accommodations that are in each individual student's IEP are being implemented correctly. Additionally, she is responsible for making sure that the students with IEPs in her classes are receiving the proper accommodations and reporting those to the other IEP teachers. To that end, June has set up a daily system in order to make sure that everyone is kept up to date of any student progress and to make sure that she keeps up with the curriculum in each of the classes that she teaches.

The next obvious question I asked her was which organizational system works the best for you? The key to her system she states is to make sure that there is one place where all the files are kept. She knows exactly where they are and always has access to them. Her curriculum files are also in a specific place enabling her to efficiently access previous lessons that can help her learn the curriculum being taught. June's final suggestion was that the administration keep inclusion and regular education teachers who collaborate well together. The classroom consistency and unified expectations benefit the students and the professionals that work with them. She emphasized keeping electronic copies of all paperwork in case the original paper copy is lost.

Empathy

Another very important characteristic a teacher must possess is empathy which the Merriam-Webster Dictionary defined as, "the action of understanding, being aware of, being sensitive to, and vicariously experiencing the feelings, thoughts, of another." Being able to empathize with our students and what they go through daily is a great way to build relationships with them. However, as with other characteristics, empathy cannot be taught in a college setting of prospective teachers. It is a quality that a person must possess or must learn before becoming a teacher. Bob Beeman, a retired elementary school social worker from Delaware, made this point to me during our interview. His job required that he meet with students on an individual basis in both their school and home settings. He stated to me that teachers need to realize what their students are going through and adjust and work with the moods that their students are experiencing and expressing. If something does not go right in the classroom because the student is facing an issue from outside the classroom and does not want to participate, the teacher has to adjust and understand that they are not causing the problem. The teacher also must be open to speaking with the student privately when they have the chance to see if they can help the student with their issue. Flexibility is critical; your lesson will not always go smoothly because student's lives do not always go smoothly.

Passion/Enthusiasm

When we are passionate about what we do, it shows; a passionate person shows enthusiasm for what they do. One summer I had to take a United States History Since Reconstruction class in order to graduate with my undergraduate degree on time. My college professor was very passionate about what he was teaching going as far as standing up on a desk in the middle of class and shouting out a speech by Abraham Lincoln. I am not advocating doing this in your classroom, but you have to admit that he was communicating excitement for his topic! Passion signals relevance and contagious curiosity about your topic and inspires learning on a different emotional level. It also shows that you are active and interactive in what you teach. And the bonus is that we are giving our students permission to be excited about what they are learning in the classroom. A passionate person finds new and alternative ways to teach their students. Standing up on a desk, may be intimidating to your students, but we might find another like explaining why Abraham Lincoln spoke the way he did or finding a shorter version of the speech that would be remembered better. The key is to contagiously communicate our love of the topic to our students.

On the flip side of the above example, Steven, a colleague of mine teaching history in a middle school in Nevada, had a professor of history who could care less about teaching. Instead of class lectures, he would lecture on the Three Stooges or what he planned on making dinner because he thought that he was a good cook. Steven related that he would talk about "his stupid wife, the stupid university, and throw erasers at us." Now, what behavior does this signal to the students? His apathy rubs off on the students and makes them care less about the course. I am sure that attendance and test scores for that class were much lower than desired.

Inspiration/Imagination

A teacher's success also pivots on the characteristics of inspiration and imagination. We have a difficult time in modern education keeping the attention span of our students especially when teachers are competing against videos, instant information, and short attention spans. We must keep in mind that slowing down the pace of information we give them will capture the attention of our students. It has been said that "one of the fastest ways for anyone to learn something is to slow down." My professor, Dr. Dan Kasambira, at Mansfield University of Pennsylvania, taught me that many years ago, and it has been my instructional mantra. To capture the imagination and attention of our students, we must use many examples that appeal to the visual, auditory, and written intellects. It is very important not to just have our students verbally acknowledge that they understand the concept, but use varying examples to help them "get the picture."

One method that I found intriguing that a colleague of mine uses is telling stories. Mary Lou Lordi, a GearUp tutor at a local high school in Allentown, PA, uses stories to capture what they are interested in. When she talks about a historical event that happened in America, she brings along pictures or videos or invites a guest speaker who is an expert to talk about the importance of the event. She simply does not lecture about it; she has the students experience the event. A couple of months ago, she put together a presentation based on her interviews with Holocaust survivors and describes the effects of the Holocaust on the victims. She brought in pictures and videos that she had collected over the years and placed them in a gallery walk. As students walked around the room to view the different stories, their imaginations opened up as they experienced the Holocaust through first-hand artifacts.

Another example to spur the imagination of our students is field trips to places that your lessons encompass. It is amazing how the students' persona changes when you take them to a place that they have never been. I remember taking students on several field trips to the Gettysburg National Park following our Civil War unit at the beginning of every year in my U.S. History class. Students do not know how vast the battlefield is and the significance of what took place there until they see it. One year, we decided to have our students experience what it was like being a soldier during Pickett's Charge and made the students run as fast as they could through the meadow where the Confederate Soldiers were ordered to attack the Union Soldiers in a last-ditch effort to win the battle. The students did not have to wear wool uniforms or carry all the equipment of a soldier, but they could not believe how far they would have to run into battle. I still have students that I am in contact with who mention to me how much they enjoyed that experience.

Intrinsic Motivation

One skill that a teacher must not only have but be able to teach their students is the ability to have intrinsic motivation. The psychological magazine, The Very Well Mind, defines intrinsic motivation as "a behavior that is driven by internal rewards." The main question here is how to change around a culture where most people seek to be rewarded by external means and to switch to rewarding themselves internally? That is the million-dollar question!

We need to start building confidence in our own abilities. A teacher becomes easily discouraged when carefully crafted plans go awry. When this happens – and it will, use the occasion to the ability to look at what went wrong and decide what you need to do to fix it. We may find that we may have to re-teach it for better understanding or fix it for future lessons. We are not going to always be the best at what we do, but we must always give ourselves permission to make a mistake, change it, and then move on. That ability is what makes us better, more confident teachers.

Our goal must be to feel and think of what we need to do to improve the greater good of our class. We discuss magical moments in a later chapter of this book, but we do not see those every day. We are helping our students experience a well-rounded education even if we never see the results of that. Not very many of our students will come back and tell us the great influence that we had on them. This would be an example of an external motivation. We must intrinsically know that we did the best we could with the available tools that we used to do the best teaching job at that time. If we can accomplish this and live by this, then we can teach our students the same skill so that they can become more effective in their lives.

Now that we understand some of the characteristics or traits an effective teacher must possess to be successful in the classroom, we are going to look at a skill that teachers must develop to be effective in our modern classrooms, creativity. We will look at how a teacher can develop creativity and still cover all of the required material.

Developing Creativity
in the Age of Standardized Testing

"Creativity is now as important in education as literacy"

— Sir Ken Robinson

Overview

Creativity is a very important skill that needs to be developed in our modern-day classrooms. Bloom's Taxonomy states that teaching creativity in the classroom is one of the most difficult skills to teach. One of the main questions I asked the teachers that I interviewed was, "how do we teach with creativity in the classroom in the age of standardized testing?" Since there are so many scripted programs available that do not provide any room for teachers to provide creativity, we need to look at some ways a teacher can be creative in his or her classroom.

Classrooms Without Creativity

There are many so many aspects of teaching that are missing if we do not include creative planning in our classrooms. We are missing an opportunity to teach the essential skills that a teacher must bring to the classroom to be successful.

Recently, I was watching the movie, "Hidden Figures," a true story based on three African-American women who were computer-like geniuses of complex math problems for the Mercury Space Program at NASA. They would compute math problems using analytical geometry for launch angles and reentry into the Earth's atmosphere to bring human space flight to America. The math for launching and reentry would change constantly. They were challenged to find ways to make the math work for the program. They had to think clearly, solve problems, collaborate with colleagues, develop new ways to help the capsule survive reentry into the atmosphere, and deal with all the obstacles of race that were common in the 1960s. Imagine if they were unable to perform these duties effectively because they were not able to use their imagination to solve the problems in front of them.

Marcia, a suburban kindergarten teacher in Hacketstown, NJ, shared with me her experience on a daily basis with her students. She has a required scripted reading program that is used in her classroom. She uses this to help her students learn the meaning of words and to read them in context. She shared with me what it is like if she does not follow the program as written in the lessons provided. "If I go off script of the program while my supervisor is there, I lose points on my evaluation. I want to be creative in the classroom because that is my nature. I am unable to do that with this program and its management." Unfortunately, her students are missing out on the skills to learn early that can help them become better and more willing students in the future. The question is how do teachers become more creative to help build skills for the students to effectively survive in today's world?

Classroom Solutions

There are many ways a teacher can take the skills that students have to learn and build on those skills to provide unique and interesting ways to teach those skills. Let's look at some ways to do this for different students at different age levels.

Autonomy

The Merriam-Webster Dictionary defines autonomy as, "a self-governing state." How does this apply to the classroom? We need to include

independent activities to have students use their brains to solve problems in the classroom. If they come up with a new concept to solve a
problem that they are reading or working on, we as teachers need to
foster that. Utilizing journals in the classroom is a great way to develop
autonomous learning within our classroom. Stacey, a 6th grade reading
teacher in a suburban school in New York State, provides us with a great
way to use journaling with the idea of using Da Vinci notebooks.

She had heard that one of her science colleagues was teaching about
Leonardo Da Vinci in his class. The students were learning that when
something came to Da Vinci's mind, he would write it down or draw it
in his journal. She began to provide time daily for her students to write
down anything that they learned during the day and to ask her questions based on their learning. She then takes the journals on a weekly
basis and attempts to answer their questions. Although this increases
her workload, she enjoys having those conversations with her students,
and they all benefit from that interaction. The journal also highlights
what the students are learning and how they apply it to their different
classes. She likes how the students open up to her about what they are
learning and how more motivated they seem to be to learn. Stacey also
commented that not only did the students keep Da Vinci notebooks, but
she started to keep one as well. It helped her remember concepts that
she was teaching in class and how to incorporate those concepts into her
teaching.

Another program that Stacey uses with her students in her 5th grade
classroom is called 1-2-3-Then Me. The basic premise of this program is
to have the students take one minute to read over the directions of the
lesson. Then take two minutes to discuss with each other what they believe is expected of them to do the lesson. Finally, they take three
minutes to develop a plan on how to complete the assignment that they
are expected to do. Stacey will not answer any questions until the first
three tasks are completed by the students. She will then be able to clarify
if students don't understand the directions or words that are confusing.

This provides independence not only in developing critical thinking skills but also providing independence in problem-solving. This is a method, like anything else, that needs to be set up and taught by the teacher so that he or she can model it for the students to then use it correctly in the classroom. Stacey stated that when she was able to provide her students with this structure not only did her test and quiz scores go up in the class by 10% - 15%, but she also noticed collaboration increased and disruptive behaviors decreased in her classroom.

Problem Solving Skills

Dependence on a teacher to solve the different problems in the classroom can be very frustrating and stressful. It detracts the teacher from providing time to focus on students who really need the help with the lesson and frustration for students who have to wait for the teacher to come over and help them. Let's look at some unique ways teachers are providing more problem-solving skills in their classroom.

One special education teacher, John, I spoke with works in a 6th grade inclusion math classroom in an inner-city school in Baltimore, MD. One of the problems he was facing with his students in the classroom was the students' dependence on him by asking too many questions during independent work and not enough time to answer all their questions. He shared with me that he now uses a classroom program with colored cups. The cups that he uses are green, yellow, and red. Each student received the three cups and placed them at their desk. The green cup tells the teacher that I am working well and do not require any help now. The yellow cup represents that I need help, but I will keep working until you are available. The red cup represents that I have stopped working and need help immediately. Using this method in the classroom enabled John to recognize which students needed help immediately and lessened their frustrating behaviors because he could answer those questions first before moving on to the students with yellow cups. John circulates the room and quickly assesses and prioritizes his energy and assistance. He stated that he became less frustrated because he did not feel that he had to rush around and answer everyone's questions all at the same time. They knew that he would be there to help them eventually depending on the color of the cups they were displaying on their desk.

Making Mistakes

One of the most invaluable ways to teach a student to become more independent and creative is to teach them that making a mistake is normal. One of the major flaws of teaching the correct answers to a standardized test is that students become frustrated quickly if they do not answer questions correctly on assignments or tests. As the frustration builds up, the student gives up because they believe the task is too difficult and cannot complete it on their own. One of the most effective math teachers that I have the privilege to work with daily, whom I had the pleasure to interview had a simple answer to this common classroom problem. Christina Kauth currently, a 9th grade high school math teacher at an inner-city high school in Allentown, PA gleaned this teaching method from her mentor when she was first teaching in Arizona. Christina has a classroom procedure poster that says, "Mistakes Are Valuable," hanging visibly in her classroom; she reinforces the message daily. The key to this short message is that we learn more effectively when we make mistakes and learn from those mistakes. Developing coping skills for students who have difficulty with this strategy is essential for them to buy what happens in the classroom. She looks for common errors that students are making, and they then discuss it as a class to see how to work through to solve the problem.

Many teenagers deal with self-esteem issues, but when they see that others are struggling with the same problem, and together, learn how to solve that problem, their self-esteem is elevated. It also provides a bond between the students and Christina in the classroom because they feel that they can solve the problems as a team instead of as individuals.

Teachers should also remember that mistakes are valuable and own up to them. That sends students the message that everyone makes mistakes, that we are all human, and that we are all learning every day.

Getting to Know Your Students' Likes and Dislikes

Being familiar with what your students like and dislike is a definite key to a fun and flexible classroom. Over the years, I have adapted my classroom lessons to include students' preferences and interests to my advantage, and although I may not particularly like what they do, I have realized this helps foster an appreciation for their generation.

For example, I noticed many students are motivated by music. A lot of them have cell phones with earbuds, and more often than not when they are not talking to their peers in the hallway, they are listening to music. They selfishly believe that their music is the best and do not think that other music is influential. So, with every decade or historical time period I teach, I play music from that period for my students. As we listen, we connect the historical context to discover why the music was inspirational or motivational to their age and talk about why the music was inspirational or motivational at that time. Music extends and clarifies historical events like Joni Mitchell's, Big Yellow Taxi, reflecting the angst over commercialism destroying nature or African American spirituals exhibiting slavery conditions. Why did Jazz become so prevalent in the 1920s? The list is endless, and it is only not only a marvelous teachable moment, but it also just might provide them with an appreciation of the music of other generations.

I was able to speak to an elementary school teacher, Adrianna, who teaches 4th grade in a rural school in Athens, PA. She shared with me a very unique strategy for her math classroom that seemed to increase academic skills and lessen disruptive behaviors in her classroom since its implementation. She finds that the students who struggle the most academically in her class are also the most artistic students in the classroom. She finds that if she discovers what they like, she can use that to help them learn to read, comprehend, and solve math problems. For instance, she had a student who was very talented in drawing, but was really struggling in math computation, especially with multiplication and division problems. She would draw small pictures representing the numbers on her worksheet. Adrianna stated that since the student learned through visual prompts, drawing the problem helped the student see the steps needed to complete the computation.

Another student in the same class who was very intelligent wanted a lot of attention and was very dramatic. She liked to be in the spotlight, and when she was not, she would act out to get that attention. Instead of scolding the student, Adrianna used the student's talent to act out stories or explain a story to others. Adrianna wisely found an outlet to release the student's energy and it turned into an advantage for the classroom as a whole.

Utilizing Open Ended Questions

During my 10th year of teaching, I attended a seminar about effective ways of teaching in a social studies classroom; one of the lectures was a discussion about the efficacy of asking open-ended questions. During this seminar, I learned that asking effective open-ended questions develops students' natural curiosity about what they were going to learn and sets up the lesson for student participation. This is especially effective when you are opening a new unit or concept within the unit. Open-ended questions provide the teacher a backdrop of student's prior knowledge level about the topic being introduced. By writing their answers down on the board or notebook and referring to them throughout the lesson to spur on more discussion, the teacher is creating a learning community where everyone learns from each other. You are sending positive signals that you are listening and responding to them.

In this strategy, I allow time for the students to respond to the question. It is important to encourage students to take time to think through their answers rather than being pushed to answer immediately. That is a problem in our society. We need to take time to think about our responses so that when we do respond, it is thoughtful and makes sense to others. It also provides us time to listen to opinions or information with which we may not agree. It gives students the opportunity to say what they feel or know. And, who knows, we just may learn something that we did not know. Asking effective open-ended questions comes down to intentional set up and monitoring.

According to to a recent article published in Desert News entitled, "COVID 19 led to 'botched" AP tests. Those tests might fix standardized tests forever," even the College Board eliminated multiple-choice questions on this year's AP tests and "included only free response questions," a move that would change the way teachers teach. No longer would we teach for understanding where students could concentrate, think carefully, and explain their answers. Teachers could then teach broad subjects and demonstrate how to answer related open-ended questions with specific examples and scenarios.

Encouraging Movement

Encouraging movement during lessons not only stimulates creativity in the classroom, but also in our teaching. Just this past year, I included more movement in my classroom by having students use gallery walks to help teach concepts. I am fortunate to teach two sections of Advanced Placement Psychology. The students were introduced to a lot of new vocabulary and new psychological concepts that students needed to learn throughout the course. In teaching, we often miss the opportunity to show how concepts are connected. Gallery walks make these connections. Students were paired together, and the class was assigned a certain concept learned in the first semester of class. They walked around and wrote on each unit poster how their concept was related to the topic taught in that particular unit. I was wondering how this would impact their understanding of everything on the mid-term final they were about to take. I graded the mid-term exam the same way the College

Board would grade the AP Exam. What I found was that the students scored mostly 3's, 4's, and 5's on the exam. I also walked by a classroom in the hallway at the end of the school day, and I noticed several of my students using this technique to teach themselves different content. It was uplifting to see them transfer this technique to their own learning process.

Providing Scenarios

I was speaking with one of my friends who is not a teacher. We were discussing three different ways I could introduce a lesson to provide an overview of World War II, and I was not sure which one would be the best one to use. The first technique was to use a basic introduction of the people, places, and turning points that made the United States become involved in the war. The second scenario was to listen to the words of the major people involved in the war, and why they wanted to become part of defeating the Axis powers. The third was for the students to share stories of what they learned from family members that were involved in the war. I tried out all the introductions on my students.

At the end of the class, students were able to share their opinions in a poll that I provided for them as an exit question. I was intrigued by their response; they stated that I should use a combination of all three introductions into one introduction. To this day, I use that combination teaching strategy as an introduction to the unit on World War II. It was an eye-opening experience for me.

How Do We Do This?

All the different techniques we discussed in this chapter must be modeled by the teacher. For creativity to flourish, the teacher is the one who must explain what creative thinking is, how it is used in the classroom, and provide examples to the students to open their minds. As a teacher, we must be open to trying new ways of teaching our students and not get into the rut of teaching the same old way day after day. If it becomes boring for us, it will be boring for our students. Remember that because we have different types of learners in the classrooms, we need to play to their strengths so that we hold their attention for longer periods of time. If we hold their attention, there is a better chance that they will learn. The longer we have their attention, the more successful we feel, and the lower the probability of disruptive behavior in the classroom.

Now that we established that utilizing lessons with creativity helps students become more involved in the classroom and develops more of a bond between the teacher and students, how do we handle the disruptive behaviors that students show in the classroom? How do we effectively redirect our students to the tasks that we ask them to complete in the classroom? The next chapter discusses ways to deal with these questions.

Dealing with Disruptive Behavior
in the Classroom

"Young people can be disruptive and screw up classes. But even if they are being a pain in the arse it's a cry for help – they don't feel like they are being listened to."

— Jamie Oliver

Overview

One of the most difficult factors to deal with in the classroom is disruptive behavior. With so many different descriptions of disruptive behaviors and different views of how and what teachers consider these behaviors to be, one would think this would not be easy to define. Simply put, The Merriam-Webster Dictionary defines the word disrupt as, "to throw into disorder." In actuality, those "disorders" have long-reaching consequences: consuming valuable class time, shifting the tone and atmosphere from certainty to uncertainty, derailing instruction, and frustrating both students and teacher. We cope with these disruptive behaviors daily in every age group and grade level ranging anywhere from speaking out of turn, yelling, biting, not following directions, refusing to participate in the lessons, not listening, running around the classroom, fighting, cursing, etc. If the behavior bothers the normal process of the classroom in the eyes of the teacher or the students, it is considered disruptive. One behavior that is considered disruptive in one classroom may not be considered disruptive in another classroom which underscores a dilemma of an all-encompassing school policy on dealing with disruptive behavior. What can we do to combat this ever-increasing problem?

Dealing with Disruptive Behavior

Several teachers interviewed provided suggestions to this ever-growing problem in our schools. When facing the many different types of disruptive behaviors, it might be wise to consult some experts. One of those experts that provided some guidance was Mrs. Molly Sinclair, who has over 22 years of experience working in the school system with various aged students. She shared one of the best ways to proactively deal with disruptive behavior in the classroom.

Classroom Structure

One of the techniques that are crucial to slow down disruptive behavior in the classroom is to provide students with a daily classroom structure. Mrs. Sinclair explained, "the key to any program becoming successful in the classroom is to implement the program consistently. If after over time we see that it is not working to decrease the behaviors that we are focused on, then we can change the program to meet the students' needs." She observed that the problem teachers face in the classroom is implementing a program, sticking with it for a while, and then dropping it when it is not working." Likewise, school districts in our country spend a lot of money on behavioral programs each year to promote learning in the classroom, but those concepts repeat the same cycle. They then keep them for a year or less, then go to another program that looks better, and try that one. Better yet, Sinclair explains the administration and teachers should effectively learn how to manage a program, develop how the classroom teachers are going to implement it, and then provide consistent consequences in the classroom and school that are followed. If there is a structural problem that the teachers or the school are dealing with, then adjustments should be made. Training should also take place throughout the year to reinforce and evaluate the program.

The cell phone concern can be managed with a very simple protocol. Require students to place their phones (on silent mode) in a charging station you strategically placed in the back of the classroom where they remain for the duration of the class period. Once they place their cell phone on that station, they should not touch it until class is over. Toward the end of class, students who comply with the program receive a ticket or a small reward for their cooperation. Several teachers interviewed have used this program and commented that it definitely curtailed cell phone use in the classroom.

Brigid Brady, a former special education teacher and current special education supervisor in southeastern Pennsylvania, stressed that the structure in the classroom should be simple and easy to understand. When the students enter the classroom each day, they should never have a question about what to expect. Even when they have expectations that might differ from ours, we should constantly reinforce and implement the classroom expectations every day. This leads us to the next important aspect in dealing with disruptive behavior consistency.

Sometimes, a solution can be straightforward, and other times it may be a bit more problematic. This was the case for Mike, a 9th grade math teacher in an urban high school in Allentown, Pennsylvania. He was informed that he would be receiving not only several classes of students who were struggling in algebra but also had many behavioral issues which decreased their attention span and learning ability. He knew that the way he taught his classes prior to this crop of students was not going to be effective. He also realized that most of these students had IEPs, Individual Education Plans, that were focused on math computation deficits. Since he was going to have an inclusion teacher in the room with these students, they collaborated to devise a classroom structure to improve the learning environment. One other note to state here, he realized that he had these students two periods per day because of their learning deficits.

What Mike did was to arrange his classroom desks into groups using his desks into stations in different parts of the room. He then looked at the grade level for math for each student and if they had any English language deficits. He grouped the students with different grade levels, including English Language Learners, and positioned himself and the inclusion teacher in different parts of the room. One station was learning about a new concept, one station was about reinforcement of skills, one was fusing the new concept with their other skills, and the final one was an extension lesson for the new concept that was learned during the class. Since they had a double period with their students, each station would be 25 minutes. Mike would focus his attention on teaching the new concepts at the one station while his inclusion teacher would be focused with the reinforcement tasks. A projection of a timer on his whiteboard indicated how much time the students had remaining at each station. As students completed each task it would be turned in at the station for later grading. The results were shocking to Mike and his inclusion teacher. Behavioral referrals were way down, the interest the students had for the subject increased because there was a good mix between instruction and independent work, and the students who were not struggling with the subject matter started helping those students who were struggling. The teacher and the inclusion teacher were free to teach and to help reinforce math skills that the students continued to struggle with.

Can you imagine an elementary school classroom without structure? Trying to corral children from the ages of 5-9 to listen, perform tasks, and complete them can be a very difficult task. Not for Angie, a 2nd grade teacher in Allentown, PA, and her class. The first thing Angie does at the beginning of the day is very simple: she meets all her students at the door with hugs, high fives, and handshakes. She has the students take their belongings and hang them in the designated area of her room. Next, they go to the book section of her room, choose a book, and then sit in that area to read for the first 15 minutes of each day. Finally, they have their morning classroom meeting and choose the jobs in the classroom for the day, and they also discuss the schedule for the day and make sure that everyone understands their schedule. She gives repeated warnings of when a transition is about to take place. This is an important point to make here. The part of the day where most behaviors occur in an elementary school setting is during transitions, especially during lunch time and going home. Even if they are working at stations for the classroom, she provides the important message of a transition approach.

What does this plan of action do for Angie? This provides her the opportunity to redirect students who are having a difficult time paying attention to their tasks. She can also focus on students' emotional or physical needs at the time when the other students are in their groups. She also understands the importance of providing breaks to use the bathroom or water fountain in their schedule. This eliminates students asking her throughout the day to use the bathroom or to get a drink. The students are aware of the schedule when these opportunities are approaching. The behaviors she used to see in the classroom are lessened. She also stated one important thing to mention here is that she needs to be flexible with the schedule and timing of when there is a change in their routine. Students need to know these changes in advance and reminders that a change is coming up. It is an effective tool that is used daily.

Consistency

Consistently implementing a program provides expectations for both teachers and students. Many students throughout the country experience instability in their home life. When they come to our classrooms, they are craving consistency. Students who are experiencing inconsist-encies at home are very good at finding loopholes in a teacher's class-room management program. Therefore, we must be consistent across the board with our programs to be effective.

Roger, a 12th grade social studies government teacher in an inner-city high school in Reading, PA provides an excellent example of why we need consistency in the classroom. An 18-year-old senior was on his phone texting his friends in class rather than taking notes as the teacher was giving a lecture a definite infraction of the no-cell-phone-out policy. Roger asked the student to put his phone away, and the student did comply for a while. Then a couple of minutes later, the cell phone was out again. After the second time, Roger asked him to put it away, the student again took it out a couple of minutes later. At this point, Roger wrote a referral to the student's assistant principal who met with the student and gave him a warning with no consequences. If the protocol was followed, the AP would have given the student at least detention after school for the actions shown in class, but he did not. Another teacher had the same problem with a student in her class, and sent a referral to another AP who assigned the student one day in school sus-pension (ISS) for the same behavior.

Without a consistent protocol with the resulting consequences when an infraction occurs as seen in the above cases, it is impossible to curtail the behavioral problems school-wide. School districts spend a lot of time coming up with policies that the students and staff must follow. If we feel like a certain program or rule is not being effective, then we have to look at that program and make adaptations that make more sense, and, thereby, increase the probability of its success rather than just not following it.

Another point to consider is consistency in the trust factor between students and teachers. Students tend to base their judgment on us based on past experiences. When we do something out of the ordinary, it makes students hesitate and think. We lose the rhythm in the classroom, and we lose a little of that trust that we have built with our students. It takes a long time for teachers to build trust with their students, and it just takes one situation where we go out of character to lose that trust.

For instance, I was having a particularly bad day. I had many things going on around me in and out of school, and I was very frustrated. I had one more class to teach that day, and I really did not feel like teaching it. Normally, I would position myself at the door greeting my students as they would enter the room. Unfortunately, right before the period started, I received a phone call from an administrator that the grant I applied for to take students on a field trip was denied. The students were puzzled because I did not greet them at the door like every other day. One student asked me several times if I was okay. Finally, after the 6th or 7th question from her, my emotions exploded out, and I yelled at her from across the room. All that pent-up emotion just came rolling out. Even though I apologized many times, it took me weeks to gain the trust and reconnect the line of communication between us. It is so important for us to be as consistent as possible because this is what our students expect.

Clear Expectations

Providing clear expectations in the classroom provides the students with a clear map of behavioral expectations. Detailed, well-explained, visible rules are easier to implement. There are a couple of principles that should be kept in mind when implementing expectations of our students in the classroom.

Expectations that are short and achievable should be posted in a classroom where everyone can view them. There should be no more than five to seven expectations written in a way that can be understood by everyone in the classroom. As previously mentioned, if agreed upon and implemented consistently, then for the most part they will be followed. If there needs to be a change to a classroom expectation, then everyone should agree upon that change.

For example, Joanne, a special education teacher at an inner-city high school in Allentown, PA, saw that a student in class was not following the expectations of handing in completed work in a timely manner. Through individual conversations with the student, Joanne found out that the student was struggling with the language in the instructions being said in the classroom. She decided to help by providing an opportunity for the student to complete assignments after the deadline by providing tutoring sessions after school. She then opened this up to the rest of the class to provide the extra help other students needed. Through conversations with the regular education teacher and subsequently the other students, provided the student and her peers an opportunity to not lose points on the assignments and turn them in on time.

Students want to know that a teacher can be trusted in their classroom to fairly oversee the expectations in their classroom; therefore, should an exception be made, students need to know why this was done without compromising an individual's confidentiality. Clear communication, addressed in more detail in Chapter 9, will build a rapport with both students and teachers to strengthen the expectations in the classroom.

A teacher should also communicate how they will respond to a student or students when an expectation is not met. Carefully anticipate and intentionally plan for this because it is inevitable that some students will put you to the test; they relish a good challenge. If a teacher responds the way students expect and hope for, teacher credibility increases, and the future tests of the will decrease.

A teacher who responds to a student in a way where the student perceives that they are being challenged rather than listened to will receive a different response from the student. For example, I once had a student in the classroom look up a fact about Abraham Lincoln on the internet. She was curious about his role in the Civil War and how he used his leadership to help the union ultimately win the war. I was teaching the class about how Abraham Lincoln would spend hours at the war department waiting for reports from his generals on the progress of battles during the war. She went on Wikipedia to find that the telegraph was not invented as of yet and showed it to me on the computer in front of her. I was able to show her the textbook and five other historical sites on the internet that showed her something different. The lesson learned is that Wikipedia gives people the opportunity to change the facts as other sites and reference books do not. I handled it in a calm, constructive manner to where other students watched as I answered her question. Through their reactions, they understood how I would answer future challenges. If I responded to her by saying, "how dare you challenge my knowledge," would have received a completely different response from the student and her peers.

How do you gain credibility with a student? An example of how this can be accomplished occurred when I first started working with Jared, a young student of whom I had little background knowledge. As a side note, sometimes, the easiest way is to get to know a student because you get an unbiased opinion about the environment and the student. When Jared and I first met, his initial reaction was, "who is this old man, and what is he going to teach me?" I rather expected that reaction from a 10-year-old viewing all the gray hair on the top of my head. After asking all the normal starter questions and discussing sports, his mom suggested that we go to the backyard to see what they had. Low and behold they had a basketball court with a hoop! Immediately, we had common ground; we both loved basketball, and we both agreed if he finished his lessons for the day, we would play basketball. This has now been successfully implemented for the past two years.

Credibility happened when I took the time to connect to the student's passion and tapped into it as an incentive.

Students Becoming Involved in the Classrooms

A well-run classroom needs to have students involved in what takes place during the time they are in the classroom. It is important to have them be a part of what you teach. I have an exercise in my AP Psychology class where student volunteers sit on a stool in front of the classroom. The idea for the lesson is to test their sensations and perceptions. I provide five different sounds and smells where the student reacts to each. Of course, the student is anxious about what is going to take place, and their peers are anxious to see their reactions. The student usually reacts to me clapping loudly right next to them, tapping them on the shoulder, or having them smell a food that they do not recognize. It is amazing after using sounds and smells to get a student's reaction to see how many students want to volunteer to be next. It is something that we do to have fun and to teach the concepts of sensation and perception.

Students have a tendency to be less disruptive in a classroom where they are more involved in the lessons being taught. In the previous chapter about creativity, we discovered that students will become more involved in lessons that are fun and challenging. For example, Kristin, run her 2nd grade elementary classroom at a charter school for students with behavior problems in Bethlehem, PA, was a master at this. When you visit her classroom, you are immediately impressed with how much the students were involved in the lesson she was teaching and how well they were paying attention. This young teacher was able to redirect the behaviors in the classroom and continue teaching to keep the other students interested in what was going on. She was able to use her tone of voice, her positioning in the classroom, her proximity down on the floor with them, and her knack for effortlessly fluently answering their questions about the book she was reading. She was in total command, yet the joy was clearly evident and contagious. This really highlights the more involved a teacher is in the lesson, the more involved the students will be involved as well.

Having a Sense of Humor

A sense of humor is an effective and disarming way for teachers to diffuse disruptive behaviors. Rather than allowing frustration to surface, redirecting the difficult situation with a bit of humor helps everyone breathe through the stress and provides a connection between us and our students.

It takes a while to develop a sense of humor in the classroom. Sometimes the things that students will do in the classroom will just make you laugh. Although I try not to show my laughter at the time because the behavior might have been inappropriate, I will chuckle later on. Once, I had a student enter my classroom and did a flip. Although, I was very impressed with his athleticism. I was not impressed because I had two student observers in the classroom at the time. So, I made him get off the floor and re-enter the room. The student observers were just waiting to see what my response was going to be. When he appropriately re-entered the room, I introduced him to the two student observers as talent scouts from the Ringling Brothers, Barnum, and Bailey Circus. We just happened to be at the end of World War I and the beginning of the Roaring 20's when he decided to do a flip. For a time, he believed they were talent scouts and wanted to do more acrobatics! The students in the classroom were laughing. He finally realized I was kidding, and he had a good laugh. This works when the teacher gets to know his students well.

Steve, a high school social studies teacher down the hallway from me at an inner-city high school in Allentown, PA, makes it a must to laugh in his classroom every day. You hear a lot of laughter coming from his room daily or when he is speaking to one of his students out in the hallway. He does try to tell jokes to the students, but he naturally has a great sense of humor. He clearly transmits the message that it is totally acceptable to be a little goofy as long as it is within the context of the class content. He sets the limits early on with his students so the humor does not get out of hand, but allowing them to lighten up a little while they are learning a new concept in class communicates that learning can be fun.

Most of all, being able to laugh at yourself when you make a mistake or to laugh at something that a student says that is appropriate makes the atmosphere more fun for you. We have students every day come into our classroom who try to make you laugh, but if it gets out of hand, redirect the conversation. Encourage humor. Every once in a while tell a joke to lighten things up, especially after a difficult test. Looking human and smiling goes a long way in connecting with our students.

Classroom Intervention Plan

How we respond to behavior problems when they first arise is key to lessening that behavior in the present moment and in the future. There are a few ideas to keep in mind when constructing a classroom intervention plan.

The first step is to understand how to utilize language when approaching a student. Keep in mind that the student is distracted, and our first priority is to redirect them to the task in the classroom. We must be non-confrontational using specific language during this step. We need to utilize functional language to intervene in these situations where disruptions occur. When a student is not on task or disruptive, we need to understand why and how this taking place. We want to avoid asking too many questions as we do not want to escalate the situation beyond where it is when we approach the student. In speaking with a student, we need to understand their needs at that moment. Once we understand the need, we provide assistance as needed to assist the student in satisfying that need. Teachers need to avoid using language that would escalate the behavior and the need for other interventions.

Paula, an elementary school teacher in suburban Canton, OH, shares how she deescalates disruptive behavior when it occurs. She states, "I realized early on that this might be caused by something that happened the night before or earlier in the day. I approach in a calm and caring way and really listen to what the student is saying." She continues, "I attempt to not approach the situation in an accusatory manner. I listen and try to support the student as much as I am able. I also redirect any spectators to not inflate the situation."

Next, if the student does not calm down or listen to what we are attempting to redirect them to, we need to provide a warning to the student that they can make a choice or we need to intervene with a choice for them. We need to choose a consequence in this instance that we can enforce. It will do us a disservice for this situation or others later if we cannot enforce the consequence we are stating. A consequence to a behavior must always be enforceable. Also, the consequence must relate the behavior being shown. It is important that they are related so that the student knows the response from the teacher. As related to the topic of consistency, we need to make sure that we utilize consequences that work, which we used in the past.

Third, if the student refuses to comply with a choice, we need to be able to deliver that consequence immediately. Depending on the behavior itself, there can be a number of consequences utilized. Some examples of these consequences may include loss of classroom privilege, you break it, you fix it, time away from the task, removal of rewards, etc... The consequences can either be positive or negative depending on the situation. We really need to get to know our students in order to be able to deliver consequences that are timely and effective.

If the behavior is consistently disrupting the classroom, we need to consult other professionals and the family to assist in developing a plan. It is important that the plan be structured and can be reinforced in the classroom. We need to be able to include rewards that reinforce the positive behavior and also an effective system to document the behavior. This can provide us with data to see if our interventions are effective.

Rewarding Behavior

Now that we understand the ways that we need to structure our room, keep the attention of our students, and redirect behaviors, how do we reward our students for what they need to do in the classroom? This is one of the most important parts of dealing with disruptive behaviors. Some experts would say that the reward of education should be enough to motivate our students to learn in the classroom. However, this is unrealistic. For example, younger students, are often unclear about whether what they are doing is right or wrong and require definite parameters to follow. And, quite honestly, our older students today are looking for affirmation and feedback for what they do. There are some great techniques that I have gleaned from other teachers to help us determine how to appropriately reward students in the classroom.

First, we do not need to positively reinforce everything that students do correctly in the classroom. It would be too time-consuming and too expensive for us to keep this up. One technique popular back in the 1960s and 1970s intended to help students stay on task and reward behavior was the token reward system. The teacher has paper cups on each of the student's desks. Every time he or she would go by their desk and the student was on task, the teacher would place a penny in their cup to reward them for their attention and good behavior. When they would get to a certain amount, the students could choose a prize from the prize box at the end of the day and take it home. If they were not behaving the way they were supposed to in class, they would have a penny removed from their cup as a punishment.

Imagine all the pennies and energy it took to continue this program every day, especially with 25 children in the classroom. Teachers would be unable to keep up with that pace. A token reward system can change behaviors but not on a whole classroom scale. We can use this for one or two of our students to change behaviors but it is not practical on a large scale.

Other teachers use a chart system in their classes. One of the classic charts that I observed in an elementary school teacher's classroom was a Stop Light System. There is a picture of a stoplight on a board in the classroom with the students' names on dots; all dots start out in the green light position at the beginning of the day. When a student needs to be reminded of their disruptive behavior, their dot or token is moved to the yellow space which means they are being warned. If their dot or token moves to the red, that means their behavior is not correct and has been warned a couple of times to change. Red also indicates that the student loses a privilege such as recess time. However, one question that comes up is if the student changes their behavior even after they have been put in the red zone of the light and were doing what they were supposed to be doing the rest of the day, should they have something taken away? In other words, were they reinforced for their good behavior even after changing it when they reached the red part of the light? This is where the teacher needs to be creative and explain to the student what they need to do and how they can earn their way back down the light to the green part of the streetlight.

Most psychologists and teachers agree that students need to be rewarded randomly. This allows the teacher to provide positive reinforcement when the student is not expecting it. Students then behave acceptably because they do not know when to expect the reinforcement. Stickers or even verbal prompts let students know that you appreciate their cooperation and attitude. We do not have to announce to everyone that you are providing reinforcement and the student on the spot. It provides a quiet, positive reinforcement for their behavior, and it allows the teacher to walk around the room and use physical proximity to prevent any behaviors from taking place. Most importantly, this gives the impression that you are aware of what is happening in the classroom in real time and that you care about what is going on. Learning is a priority for us, and it will be for them as well.

Patti, an elementary school teacher in Witchita, KS, provides an example of how she uses this program in her classroom. Patti walks around the room throughout the day with green stickers in her pocket. When she notices one of her students showing appropriate behaviors, she will walk by the desk of the student and place a green sticker on the desktop. When a student receives five randomly placed green stickers, they receive a prize of a small toy that they choose at the end of the day. Once these stickers are given, they are not taken away. A student can then earn more stickers beyond the first five. She states, "they do not know when they will receive them, and I use proximity in the room to identify those students who receive the stickers. It has really changed their behaviors, and I feel that I have more time to teach concepts rather than correcting their behaviors."

Documentation of Behaviors

How we document behaviors in order to receive help from administrators and families that may or may not provide a clearer explanation of what is going on in a classroom. Our documentation must unmistakably show a pattern of behavior and the exact steps we have taken to decrease the disruptive behavior. This provides a paper trail that validates what we have with the students when an issue occurs. One uncomplicated but very effective documentation which records behaviors and pinpoints patterns is the A+B=C method..

The A part of the behavior equation is the Antecedent, or what takes place before the behavior begins. It questions whether there was something going on in the classroom or school environment that could have triggered the student to have a certain behavior. Was the behavior prompted by something said to the student, was the room too hot, or was the student tired or hungry when you approached them? The antecedent looks at many different avenues that can describe what may have triggered the behavior to happen.

The B in the equation stands for Behavior. This is the actual behavior that took place. We must be able to document the actual behavior and its frequency. Use as many adjectives as possible to describe the behavior, and if possible compare these behavioral occurrences at specific times during the day or in certain settings. This will match the behavior with the Antecedents to see if there are any patterns.

The C in the equation stands for the Consequences that were done after the behavior occurs. What did we do or others in the classroom do in response to the behavior? These responses are usually unscripted because they are responses to the actual behavior. This can be the student receiving a negative response from someone, such as someone yelling at the student, striking them, or getting a negative response from the teacher. It could also be a response that reinforces the behavior when other students laugh or encourage the behavior. This should be documented as well so that we can see if anything we are doing, or others are doing in the classroom environment that may be causing the behavior to occur or reoccur.

How can these categories of the behavior be documented? You can look on the internet for already made three column charts that outline the three different sections of A+B=C, or create your own by folding a plain piece of paper into three sections. The sections at the top are labeled with the corresponding letters for the equation. Remember if we do not document what took place in the classroom, the behavior never took place.

The gain from the analysis of this data is to see if there are certain triggers or responses that can be changed to decrease or eliminate the behavior altogether. It provides not only documentation of what has occurred, but it also gives the professionals in the building a non-biased look at what is taking place with the student. This documentation should be taken over a week's period time to provide an accurate account of the behavior.

Clearly, there are more good teaching practices a teacher can initiate in order to deal effectively with disruptive behavior in the classroom in addition to this overview. Dealing with individual behaviors within that framework needs an individual response from the teacher to address it. Show leadership in the classroom as you set up structure, consistency, and rewards for a highly effective classroom. We will define and provide examples that are key to being a leader in the classroom in the next chapter.

The Teacher as a Classroom and School Community Leader

"If your actions inspire others to dream more, learn more, do more, and become more, you are a leader."

— President John Quincy Adams

Overview

A teacher is a natural leader. In a description of a teacher, we use words like supportive, enthusiastic, helpful, and prepared. Leadership is a description generally not used. If you think about it, teachers are the first people we meet, outside our parents, that are true leaders. Many people want to emulate their teachers and remember how a teacher molded leadership characteristics within us. There are many examples of former teachers who went on to be famous leaders including, Moses, Aristotle, President John Adams, President Lyndon Johnson, and President Jimmy Carter, to name a few. There are some skills that a teacher needs to attain in order to be an effective leader in the classroom. We will discuss several different skills needed in order to be a classroom and community leader.

Model an Attitude to Work Hard

One of the skills that a teacher needs to be a leader is to have the attitude to work hard at teaching. We must be able to model how hard we would like each student to work in our class. We say to students quite a bit that we are going to work hard for them to succeed, but if we are working harder than they are working, there is an imbalance. For the first month, it is suggested that we model to our students how hard we want them to work. Provide them with the expectations; let them know that you have seen their past academic and behavioral records and have a background of what they do well and do not do well. Have high expectations because if we lower them too far, our students become bored and disinterested in what we are trying to teach.

Model how our students earn their grades and achievement in the classroom. Telling our story of how we were able to get to the point in our lives to earn the right to teach in the classroom is always a good place to start. Tailor that story to the age of our students and show you succeeded in getting to this point in your life. For most of us, it was a difficult journey in order to earn the right to be a teacher. Sharing that story and modeling it in the classroom is a powerful way to communicate how to work hard to achieve your goals.

Identifies Leaders in the Classroom and Cultivates Their Abilities

A teacher needs to be able to identify the natural leaders in each class and utilize their skills to help the class. When we see a leader, cultivate that ability. Great leaders utilize the gifts of their students to make the class run more smoothly and reduce the stress of the overall leader. Emphasize such concepts of a good leader as being goal-oriented, honest, willing to help others, making good decisions, optimistic, and taking responsibility for their actions and work. These are concepts that we can write into a lesson plan, but we can make them a part of our classroom. The burden of the class should not always be all on the teacher. If we were running a business, it would not be very successful if our workers did not believe in what we are attempting to produce or accomplish. The same thing goes for the classroom. We have objectives to attain and learn and students need to be a part of that. Setting up our students to be leaders makes us better teachers and leaders.

How do we accomplish this in the classroom? Assign jobs daily so students begin to feel they are an integral part of the classroom. Taking a job seriously and taking ownership of their job not only makes the routine run smoothly but also increases student motivation and interest. Students who read well should be encouraged to read to the class. Students who are social should be encouraged to write at the board or explain tasks to other students who are struggling. This frees up time for the teacher to deal with behavioral issues, on task behaviors, or students who need the most academic help. It also shows that we trust our students to help in the classroom, and trust builds a bond between the teacher and students.

Amaris Recker, a Spanish teacher in an urban high school in Allentown, PA tells us how she finds leaders in her classroom. She states, "I choose leaders very carefully. I observe how they interact with others, if they lead by example, and how they interact under stress in the classroom." This provides her information to see the students who are able to lead and include others in making decisions in the classroom. She states one more aspect that a classroom leader must possess: "Leaders don't have to be fearless but shall be able to conquer their fears." This provides students with confidence in themselves and increases their self-esteem.

The Teacher is Responsible for Final Decisions in the Classroom

A teacher is ultimately responsible for what takes place in the classroom. We must get away from the notion that the classroom is a democracy. It is most certainly not. We naturally want to include our students in the decision-making process of the classroom, but the final decision in anything that takes place in the classroom falls on the teacher. We need to be role models for our students in that sense. We need to model for them how a good decision is made and the steps that are necessary in order to come to that decision. Likewise, we must model how to own up to our mistakes and how to correct them. Later in this chapter, we will discuss this dilemma of what you do when you make a mistake.

One middle school special education facilitator, Jennifer, who works in an urban district in Allentown, PA had a great idea on how a teacher can be a good final decision-maker. The situation she described to me was regarding a former student that she taught in a 9th grade high school English class where she started her teaching career. Too often, we miss small cues that can help our students become successful because we all like to have the status quo. This student was diagnosed with autism and was really struggling in her regular education placement. Jennifer describes the decision to bring the student back to her learning support class in order to see what was going on with her. The student had a fear of being in the classes without support, but she had a difficult time expressing those feelings. Once Jennifer had time to figure out what was going on, she helped the student become successful in her class, and then had her placed in inclusion classes with another special education teacher. The success of her student continued in the inclusion classes. The student was able to graduate with honors. Sometimes we must go the extra mile to discover what is really going on and make critical decisions to change the pattern. A good leader takes responsibility for what goes on within a classroom and makes carefully considered options and changes based on observations in the classroom.

Roles in the Classrooms

A teacher needs to set the roles that each person will perform in the classroom early. There should be no role confusion, and students need to know that the classroom environment is one of collaboration and learning. Effectively, students should know what they need to do when they enter the classroom. Teachers want to avoid the pitfall of students believing that they are in charge of what happens in the classroom. The teacher sets the tone early that their classroom will be a warm and inviting place for the students to be a part of. Students will learn how to be leaders in the classroom through well-defined roles that are set up by the teacher. The role students is defined by them being inquisitive, active participants, contributing to the class culture, and having personal accountability. Teachers develop plans that provide guidance on the roles in the classroom and how those roles are divided. Through careful planning and buy in from the students, the classroom will run smoothly.

Judy Davis, a teacher in the Culpepper County Public Schools in Virginia, states that a teacher must set the tone on what the different roles are in the classroom at the beginning of the year. Through encouragement and guidance, we can show our students what the roles are in the classroom and have them develop leadership skills in the classroom within that framework. Her husband, Ken, a special education teacher in the Prince William County Schools also in Virginia, works with his classroom staff to set the standards to be followed based on the students' likes and dislikes. This helps set the goals for each individual student and shows that everyone plays a valuable role in the outcome of the objectives set in the classroom. Both of these teachers have learned defining the roles in the classroom is valuable.

A Leader Admits When They are Wrong

One of the things that a good leader does in the classroom is to admit when they are wrong; it is difficult to admit wrong-doing because we try very hard to be as precise and correct as possible in front of the students. Yet, contrary to our perception that we have failed, students will actually respect you own up to your mistake. Let's explore why we need to be able to do this as teachers.

First, teachers need to realize that admitting mistakes shows strong character. If you have come to the realization that you are incorrect about something or a mistake was made, there is a strong possibility that others will already have noticed it. In the short term after the mistake has been made, students will remember that you made the mistake.

However, over time, they will realize your integrity and leadership. Society would rather have a leader who grew professionally from making that mistake rather than someone who makes mistakes and changes nothing.

Human beings have that desire inside to not fail. Just as our students do not want to fail, teachers do not want to fail. Being mistaken or wrong about something in class does happen from time to time. Just as our students need to understand that it is more about the process to get to an answer, we need to understand where we made the mistake and change that process. We need to teach ourselves that the best part of making mistake in fact or judgment is not making it but getting back up and changing it for the future. Remember it is not how many times we fall, but how many times we get back up.

In reality, people who never admit that they were wrong are not strong but weak. Always being right is merely a false excuse to prop up ego and insecurities. A stronger personality can take the temporary hit to their ego and become stronger because of it. We need to let our students know that being wrong may be a short time hit to their self-esteem, but ultimately they will bounce back more knowledgeable and have higher self-esteem. I will admit that I made quite a few mistakes when I first became a teacher, but I am a better teacher now because of those mistakes. Every time I make a mistake, I made a note in my plan, instructions, or wherever I made my mistake so that I do not repeat it in the future.

Finally, not being able to admit that you are wrong damages the link that we have between ourselves and the students. The students are very good at noticing when you make a mistake and are more than willing to point it out to us. At first, we can be defensive as we silently absorb a very big shock to our self-esteem. Understand not admitting the mistake is what the students will remember, probably not the mistake. This will damage the teacher-student relationship and become a long-standing classroom problem. However, when admitting we were wrong will reverse that feeling in the long run, leaving students with increased respect and an indelible example of responsibility, maturity, and leadership. A secure bond of trust will be developed between you and your students.

A Classroom Leader Challenges Students to Think

An effective leader not only models responsible actions but also, challenges our students to think. Just as there is always an opportunity for us to learn something new, there is always an opportunity for our students to learn something new as well. Whether it is a new concept, a way to expand overall knowledge, or to think differently about something, we need to encourage new ideas. In a recent class that I was conducting online, I was teaching my students how to process new information into an essay-formatted answer. My job is to have them think of a way to articulate their answers concisely and thoughtfully. My students in my AP Psychology classes are smart and can find answers sometimes before you are even done asking the question. What they struggle with is answering free response questions and writing their responses in a cohesive way. I have been spending time with them on not only getting the answers correct but also writing them in a uniform way as they answer the question. Without writing in a uniform way, the answer seems unorganized. By pointing out how to change their answer to make it easier for someone to read, they see how they can answer the question more efficiently and differently than in their previous response. It is refreshing to see them latch on to a new way of learning of approaching free-response questions and adjust their writing process accordingly.

Continuous Learning

A final aspect of what makes an effective leader is to continue learning how to teach and advance our subject knowledge. Why is this important? Students need to learn that teaching or learning never stops in anyone's life regardless of our age and experience and that life is a journey of continuously learning new concepts and new ideas. The most effective leaders in the industry include those that can teach as well as lead, and to that, they continue to investigate new ideas in their expertise. There will always be a situation that needs to be solved or something that needs to change in a better way, and to always assume that we have the answer makes us obsolete. Never stop learning how to present material in a better and different way if it helps our students learn. Every situation we encounter provides an opportunity for us to teach our students something new, and often, for us to learn something new about our students. They do not come to us with questions about academics but often embed questions in conversations about personal relationships, troubles outside school, or issues with other students. Opportunities to give suggestions of other possibilities or other alternative ideas may just affect the way they make decisions in the future. These are life-learning lessons that can be even more life-changing than just the facts and concepts of class lessons.

Leadership is an important aspect of being a teacher. We need to develop these skills early in order to be successful at what we do; a powerful aspect of a good leader is being a good planner. In the next chapter, we will discuss ways a teacher can be a very good planner that leaves nothing to chance.

Don't Leave Anything to Chance

"By failing to prepare, you are preparing to fail."

— Benjamin Franklin

Overview

The National Science Board in 1999 had a quote about one of the most important qualities a teacher to possess. They wrote:

Public opinion overwhelmingly favors "ensuring a well-qualified teacher in every classroom as the top educational priority. Indeed, teachers, once viewed as central to the problem of student undera-chievement, are now being recognized as the solution. In teacher preparation, there is a "multiplier effect" that can span generations. While a sound undergraduate science education is essential for producing the next generation of scientists, it is equally essential for future science teachers. The refrain, "You can't teach what you don't know," surely applies.

Surely this concept applies to any of the teaching disciplines in our schools today. There is absolutely nothing that can replace a well-prepared teacher, and students can readily distinguish between a prepared and an unprepared teacher. An unprepared teacher has to constantly refer to the book, a textbook, a reference book, or the internet to answer students' questions because they do not understand the material well. Understand, this is not implying we have all the answers and will research to discover the correct information, but too much downtime designated to check information that is an integral part of the lesson leads to decreased student attention, an increased chance of disruptive behavior, a confusing teaching style, and a lack of continuity for subsequent lessons.

Lesson Planning

A smart, skilled teacher will have unit lesson plans with an end in mind to not only to test the students effectively, but to also foster a cohesive flow in the classroom. Megan, a colleague of mine and an English teacher and department head at an inner-city high school in Allentown, PA, uses a monthly teaching calendar that she provides to the students. Now, this can be adapted to the internet if you use programs like Google Classroom. She states that the calendar allows the students to preview what types of lessons they will be learning and note the dates of the assessments throughout the unit. Megan includes students' birthdays on the calendar. This personalized touch shows how much she cares about her students as they hit their milestones during the year. Even if there is something that interrupts that schedule such as a snow day or school event, the dates can always be adjusted. If the calendar is posted on the school website, the teacher can always post the modified schedule for the students and parents. Planning the unit with the ending in mind indicates that the teacher is in control of the curriculum, is focused and knowledgeable, and is taking into consideration the pace of learning in the classroom.

The calendar is a great idea, but what about preparing the lessons for each of the days on that calendar? Another suggestion from another colleague, Dan Jurasits, a social studies teacher at an inner-city high school in Allentown, PA, includes a weekly planning outline that goes with the monthly calendar provided to the students. Each day is planned out with the objective, state standard, opening, body, and assessment for each of the lessons. He usually plans out one to two weeks in advance and provides our supervisor a copy if requested. It is more open-ended to allow for creativity within the lesson and to meet the needs of each of the different classes. Remember, that each class that we teach will have its own personality, issues, and differences that a teacher must anticipate. Again If there are any variations in the calendar, then the weekly lessons can be adjusted to meet the change in the schedule.

Planning for Absenteeism

Depending on where you teach and how it is handled, absenteeism can be a problem. Where I teach, students miss an average of 10 – 30 days per school year putting them at a high disadvantage compared to students who attend daily. There are some simple programs that we can put into place for chronic absenteeism.

One of the things that I instituted into my classroom was a staple folder for each class that I teach on the bulletin board by the door to my classroom. If a student misses a lesson, then I write their name on top of the paper or lesson that they miss, and it is placed in the class folder. When they return, they can pick up their missed work. When a student is absent for a longer period, I have a copy of the worksheet or lesson on my computer and send them an email with the missing lessons attached. Because of the COVID-19 pandemic, I set up a Google Classroom account for all of my classes and provide the assignments daily on that site. Students can complete them and submit the assignments during their absence or bring them in when they return. Both the folder method and Google Classroom approach reduce the excuse factor.

Another program that helps to deal with absenteeism in the classroom is the Remind App, an application is set up with each individual and parent through a cell phone number or email account. A message is sent out to everyone signed up with an account reminding them of an assignment, quiz, or upcoming test. It will help students who are absent to keep up with work that is missed, keep the parents in the loop, and open communication with the teacher.

It is an amazing fact to notice how much faster the day goes by when we have planned well. For example, there is a marked difference in a school day when I am teaching a lesson versus the days that I am giving a test to the students. When monitoring a test, a teacher has to constantly watch the clock to monitor how much time is left for the students to complete the test. Staring at a clock definitely makes the period or the day drag on. Yet, when you are teaching a lesson, time seems to fly. This also applies to teachers who are prepared. When there are gaps in the lesson, we tend to stare at the clock to see how much time is left for the instruction we are providing. One suggestion about surviving test days, the teacher is for the teacher to have something to grade, plan, or do while the students are taking the test so your focus is shifted to accomplishing something other than clock-watching.

Classroom Set-up to Meet the Needs of Your Students

Knowing your students is the key to a functional classroom set-up, and it makes a significant difference in your effectiveness. Anticipating the needs of those in our classes prior to the lesson will give us a major advantage that puts us ahead of the game. Although there are several different techniques to achieve this, a memorable, personal story is the best illustration.

One time in my career, I had a student who needed to move around the room constantly. No matter what type of redirection or proximity control I used, it did not work. Not surprisingly, the student was not doing very well in my class. I structured a plan to help him not only deal with the amount of energy that he had but also give him the opportunity to complete his assignments. I set up two desks for him in the classroom. When he felt the need to get out energy, he could walk over to the other desk that he was assigned, do the work there, and then return to the other desk when he needed to get up and move again. When he completed the assignment, he wrote his name on both papers, stapled them together, and handed them in. What I realized was literally how bright he actually was, and once we dealt with his need to move around and not be disruptive to other students, he was able to excel.

The way the classroom is physically set up for the needs of your students and planned accordingly. I have observed many cluttered classrooms where there was inadequate room to move around, or so much stuff lying about that the room almost felt confining. Physical clutter competes for our students' attention, makes them less productive, and gets them off task. A well-prepared teacher should understand how to organize the environment and information in a way rather than obstructs student learning. Should I have tables for my science class or have desks? Should I have rows of desks or should I have a configuration that gives me access to all my students in the classroom? Currently, I have a rainbow design for my desks in the classroom and keep the lane in the middle open. There is enough space in between for students to walk to their desks and have access to supplies that they need in the classroom. This setup focuses the attention of the students on the middle of the classroom, especially during any lectures or instructions. Furthermore, students are not staring at the backs of other students' heads. I think of it like a seesaw. Setting up the classroom design effectively is like a seesaw. The middle of a seesaw is known as the fulcrum and provides the balance when two equal weights are sitting on each side of the seesaw. Likewise, a classroom should be balanced with the same number of students on each side of the teacher like the fulcrum in the middle.

New Teachers Spend Time Planning and Teaching in the First Couple of Years

In the first few years of teaching, a teacher may feel overwhelmed with all the time spent on teaching and planning. If a teacher would keep a binder for each of the classes taught, including the lesson plans, worksheets, assignments, assessments, calendars – everything we use, we will have future access for planning. Be sure to add personal notes on what did not work well, what could have been done better, or how the lesson could be improved. If possible, take time to make those changes in your plans to save time later. Of course, we will need to change and adjust any standard or informational changes as needed. Once we have these archived, we can easily adapt the lesson plans based on the needs of the students in the classroom, but leave the framework intact. Teachers will have more time to learn about the content, add artifacts, find creative avenues, and provide more expertise for future lessons. This takes time and effort, but teachers will be saving time in the long run and not planning hurriedly to meet the criteria of the lessons.

New teachers are more effective when the lessons are going to be taught are practiced and timed before the students hear it for the first time. Why is this important? First, the teacher can gauge how much time will be needed to go through the lesson. Then, and probably most important, add in time for interruptions, questions, and distractions because those will inevitably happen especially if it is not planned. However, develop a backup plan with an extension activity to develop higher thinking skills and/or extra content related to the lesson in case there are no class interruptions in the class, and there is extra time at the end of the period. This may be an opportunity for students to begin an assignment connected to the lesson and provide a window for you to walk around and ask questions.

I understand that the next suggestion seems very simple, but pre-reading and previewing student material is an indispensable step for classroom control. Make sure that the chapter or readings are being prepared for the lesson and understand the questions that go along with the assignment. More often than not, students do not have an understanding of the initial wording of questions or their relevance. Understand the language and phraseology in case a question needs to be restated in a more understandable context. The students then can view the teacher as an expert on the topic and feel confident to answer student questions. Helping students to understand the context builds rapport and building rapport develops active learners.

Student Organization

Students of any age need organization just as much as the teacher does. Just as we use binders and notebooks to keep our lessons organized, each student should have a notebook, binder, or container to keep their papers manageable. Teachers need to model this for it to be effective. An unorganized teacher silently gives students permission to be unorganized as well. Students are naturally unorganized and need help finding ways to help them organize not only their papers but also their thoughts. Along with a place to keep important papers, each student needs a checklist of work that needs to be completed. This list gives the student an idea of assignments that have been completed and clearly shows which ones have not been completed or missing grades. If students have questions, or if they have been absent they can simply look at the checklist and see what needs to be completed. A checklist encourages students to learn responsibility for their own work without relying on the teacher for all of their missing information.

It is important to note that a teacher must exercise flexibility when helping students become organized. Some students might resist the methods that we come up with in the classroom, so it is important to give the students options to show that there is more than one way to be organized. Computers can also organize our students utilizing different tools like Google Classroom, which can keep students organized without needing a place to organize physical papers.

Strive to Reach All Students

Finally, a teacher who is prepared understands that there will be students who go above and beyond to do well, ones that struggle but work hard, and ones that will not want to try or be motivated to complete work. Be prepared to develop plans and classroom structure that deals with the different types of students. Provide enhanced learning opportunities for our overachievers and challenge their minds. Provide as much assistance and support to our students who work hard but need extra explanations for understanding. But, those students that are not motivated need the most attention. We can help unmotivated students through our organization in the classroom.

First, understand what type of learner these students most closely resemble and focus instructions and our assignments to fit that learning style. This will play to their strengths, so they believe that the assignment is much easier than it seems.

Next, we need to take the focus for these students off extrinsic motivation no matter how much we would like to use it. The more that we use this type of motivation the more the student will shut us out making it more difficult for the assignments to be completed. Focus your instruction on intrinsic motivation where the student understands the result of the assignment and how it will benefit them.

Earlier in this chapter, we discussed that a well-defined routine will help students focus, especially those who are unmotivated. Focus the instruction on understanding the important words in a lesson, provide friendly competition between students, or provide a closing question that must be answered before the end of the class.

Providing private, confidential individual attention where appropriate shows the student that you believe they are important. If a teacher does this in a more public, obvious setting, the student may shut down emotionally. Offering a couple of minutes of attention on a one-on-one basis during our class time will motivate and encourage them.

Finally, assigning unmotivated students a job that is exclusive to them with a sense of belonging in the classroom. Knowing how they learn can buy them into a class project or game; using their strengths could help struggling students understand the content better than our explanations. Over the years, I have discovered that some of the most unmotivated students that I taught were the smartest in the class. If we can catch their attention by giving them responsibility, they might just start trusting us. Once a bond and trust are established, motivation and completed work may follow.

Now that we have looked at planning for our students, recognized how important it is to be prepared in our lesson planning, and realized that we need to intentionally set up our classroom, we need to be able to communicate those lessons effectively. The next chapter dives into the subject of how a teacher needs to effectively communicate with the students as well as one another.

Teachers Need to Be Effective Communicators

"First learn the meaning of what you say, and then speak."

— Epictetus

Overview

Being able to communicate clearly to students, families, and administration is essential for a teacher's successful career. This chapter will focus on the do's and don'ts for effective communication and what is the best way to communicate with other teachers, administration, and parents within our building and community. We will look at what it means to be an active listener in the classroom, and the steps a teacher needs to take to become that active listener. Finally, we will look at what a teacher needs to do to communicate instructions to the students in order to lower the stress level in the classroom.

Dos and Don'ts of Effective Communication

It is very important to be able to communicate effectively with the people that we work with on a daily basis. Building those positive relationships with our colleagues encourages collaboration and discussions when any issues that come up during the day need to be dealt with competently. That being said, what should we avoid doing when communicating, and then what we can do to build professional relationships.

Good communication means avoiding discussing other teachers with your students as this really undermines the authority that the teacher has with the students. It also diminishes any authority and trust with our students; if another teacher becomes part of the discussion, students could well assume that they will also be discussed. We cannot teach our students to not talk about each other when we are bad-mouthing another teacher. This hypocritical example gives the impression that we do not care about others.

Equally important in effective interaction is to avoid discussing our colleagues with parents or guardians. This can cause significant problems in credibility for that teacher as well as our own. This can cause a hostile work environment especially if that parent should happen to speak with the other teacher. This would inevitably lead to a rift with the other faculty member and prevent further collaboration. Imagine the mistrust and animosity this practice could generate throughout the school.

A third area to avoid participating in gossip or hearsay which also sparks an atmosphere of misinformation and mistrust. A teacher has enough classroom drama to deal with on a daily basis without worrying about what other teachers are saying behind their back. With teaching as stressful as it is, we need to be supportive of our colleagues and be proactive by making it clear to faculty, students, and parents know that we do not want to be known as a rumormonger. Being proactive lowers stress levels and increases the mental energy needed to interact with the students and colleagues successfully.

A fourth area to circumvent would be to never confront another faculty member in front of students. This is a bad precedent to set. It not only shows how unprofessional we are, but it also models for the students to handle differences and controversy. Students are always watching how we act, and they emulate what we do. If we have a conflict with another teacher, wisely hold the conversation until there are no students present and calmly talk through the difference of opinion.

Knowing not what to do leads us to discuss the beneficial skills needed for constructive communication. Everyone wants to feel that they belong and teachers are no different when it comes to their working environment. The positive feeling of being a part of a family-like lowers stress. Spend time discussing topics that interest your colleagues and make them feel valued. This building block establishes connections and forms bonds that go beyond the classroom.

Good communication is dependent on an operable chain of communication in the school. It is really important for staff to know who to talk to and the appropriate time to talk about it. It is unprofessional to email or text a supervisor during class time; unless it is an emergency, continue and wait until after the period ends to contact your supervisor to schedule an appointment.

Connecting and communicating regularly provides an opportunity to meet with one another and discuss issues or teaching techniques that are working within the framework of the school. One of the things that we discussed earlier was that teachers should not feel isolated. Isolation increases our stress levels and makes us feel that we do not matter to others.

Finally, notice a colleague or staff member in the school is going above and beyond normal parameters in teaching or is trying to reach their students in a unique way. Let them know how important their actions were and how much we appreciated what they did. We all like affirmation that what we are doing is worthwhile. Praise increases energy, produces smiles, provides incentives, and boosts morale. Furthermore, it is contagious! We will discuss later in Chapter 13, and why this is important.

Active Listening

Being able to listen to others is another important component of a school's success. We often get so busy throughout the day in completing many different tasks that we often find ourselves thinking more, talking over others, and listening less. We have to slow down our thinking in order to listen effectively. Otherwise, we are hearing words, not ideas or concerns. How many clues do we miss out on when we forget to listen? How do we build active listening skills in a busy classroom environment? There are some outstanding techniques to increase our active listening skills.

To be a good listener, we need to suspend judgment when someone is speaking to us and not jump to any conclusions. Avoid thinking about our response based on early preconceptions and really listen closely and intently to what the person is trying to say. This way nothing is blocking or interfering with the communication link between the people involved in the conversation.

Second, we must focus on the person speaking. Make continual, deliberate eye contact still noticing the speaker's non-verbal cues and posture as they are talking. This indicates that we are really listening to them and gives us additional cues to their meaning. Keep in mind our tone of voice and how we answer questions are important. We need to remain in a neutral position and encourage the person to express themselves and provide a non-judgmental atmosphere to encourage complete communication.

Third, do not interrupt during the conversation. Nothing shows disinterest and detachment more than if we are answering emails or the phone, grading papers, or doing other tasks. In the fast-paced world today, it is important to focus without interruption on the speaker. If we need to, ask permission to jot down some notes the person is trying to communicate. Not only will that keep us busy but also indicates true concern and interest in what they are saying.

Finally, it is important to have pause time before responding to the other person's questions. We really need to give considered thought to what the person is asking us to respond to. It is important to be sure that the person is completely finished before asking clarifying questions. This shows the person that we are trying to be thorough and honest in responding to them and interested in what they have to say and that you were really listening. When we respond, continue holding your eye contact. This can also provide you time to summarize what the other person is saying to reaffirm their communication.

Clear Communication

In Chapter 7, "Dealing with Disruptive Behavior," we discussed the importance of how a teacher must have clear expectations in the classroom. Clear expectations must be stated in simple terms so that everyone understands what they need to do. In this section of the chapter, we will discuss how a teacher can establish well-defined parameters to ensure that students understand what they need to do.

Clear communication requires students to listen, so we need to be able to establish the difference between hearing and listening. When someone is listening, they are paying attention to what is being said. Hearing is basically collecting data; however, we must be able to respond to the data with a logical connection. Getting our students to listen to us can provide a logical chain of what we would like to communicate.

Second, clear communication does not always happen when the teacher positions themselves in the front of the classroom. It has actually been shown that students become more involved in what is going on in the classroom depending on the position of the teacher, so if we occasionally move around the room, students will have to shift focus. This provides the students with a classroom atmosphere that facilitates increased participation and attentive listening to what the teacher is trying to communicate. It also provides the teacher with control of the classroom using proximity control.

Next, a clear communicator needs to be aware of their pace of speaking. When we have a tendency to speak quickly, often because we are so intent on getting through the lesson, students have difficulty following and will effectively tune us out. This is especially relevant when we are teaching students who have a special education designation or who are learning English as a second language. When we recognize glazed-over looks and fidgety body language, we need to slow our speaking pace to give every student time to process what we are saying.

Finally, clear communication allows us to encourage more positive feedback from our students. Why is the clearest communication we give in the classroom often a response to negative behavior? Instead, open up conversations in the classroom that reinforce or re-state lesson objectives and key information. Ask extension questions, application scenarios, or use visual prompts that will indicate whether true listening and understanding have happened. In other words, listen to them as if they were listening to us. Opening up conversations in the classroom rather than having one person doing all of the talking dramatically increases the learning curve.

Up to this point, we have laid the groundwork for us to become effective teachers. Through being aware of the characteristics are an effective teacher, developing skills to become more creative in the classroom, lowering disruptive behaviors in the classroom, becoming a leader in the classroom, effectively planning lessons, and learning to be a clear communicator with active listening, we are laying the building blocks of an enjoyable, well-run classroom that shapes active learners and successful teachers.

Yet, there are more questions that we need to answer in the final section of the book. What is a teaching life like? How can a teacher balance their career and their home life? And, we want to encourage you with inspirational stories from other teachers who have survived those rough days, weeks, months, or years that many of you may be (or will be) facing.

Part III:
The Teaching Life

The Balance

"Most of us spend too much time on what is urgent and not enough time on what is important."

— Stephen R. Covey

Overview

There is a misguided notion in society that we teach school because we have all this time off for holidays and the summer. In far too many conversations over the years, this "perk" is inevitably brought up by those who do not work in our career choice. Ironically, if this were the reason for teaching, our profession would be flooded with more teachers! The reality is that we spend a lot of our time grading, planning, and completing seminars required to keep our teaching certificates current. Many teachers are forced to bring a good amount of their work home with them because there is simply not enough time during the school day to accomplish all we need to finish, to connect with our students, to assume assigned duties like bus duty, hall, cafeteria, or playground monitoring, study hall supervision, etc. In this chapter, we will focus on how teachers can manage their time better while in school and discuss how teachers can effectively balance their time between family and school.

Time Management Skills

William Penn, the original founder of the Commonwealth of Pennsylvania, wisely said in a very poignant statement, "Time is what we want most, but what we use worst." We spend a lot of time putting out fires during the day and wonder where all the time went with all the work we still must complete. We, as teachers, must be really skilled at managing our time. Otherwise, we will be overwhelmed with what we do on a daily basis. Discovering different ways that a teacher can use to effectively manage our time on a daily basis during the school year will greatly reduce stress and increase productivity.

The first skill that a teacher must master is being able to organize your day-by-day priorities. Teachers need to be able to arrange their daily tasks that have the most impact. Focus on tasks that must be completed on a daily basis first by preparing and making sure that our lessons are ready for our students, that worksheets, copies, and Power-Point presentations are ready to be seen, and that your classroom is set up for student learning. Make sure we have included time planned into each lesson to answer student questions and to collect student work. Never forget to plan time for yourself. Many of the teachers that I teach with make sure that they schedule alone time during the school day to enjoy some quiet time. We encourage our students to do that, and we should encourage everyone we work with to do the same thing. It is essential that we have time to unwind during the day; otherwise, we do not get time to do this, we become overwhelmed and frazzled.

Another skill that would save us time in our teaching life is to have students complete repetitive work for homework. Asking students to practice concepts outside the classroom, online or in paper form, is a better use of limited time in the classroom. Use our classroom environment for instruction of concepts, practice for the new information, and then test the memory and the ability of our students. Additionally, this allows more time for actual teaching and correction of concepts that seem difficult for our students to grasp. If a student continues to have difficulties with the concepts they have to complete at home, provide tutoring time to see where the difficulty lies student and provide re-teaching.

A third suggestion for teacher time management would be to chunk grading papers and tests. Chunking involves breaking down tasks into smaller, more manageable tasks. With grading instead of attempting to grade everything at once, break it down into smaller chunks of time rather than doing it all at once. For instance, if you teach six classes, and you must grade the tests by this week, grade them by class for the five days of the week. If you grade two periods on Monday and one period for the next four days, you still provide the test grades by the end of the week but spend less time daily grading the tests. With another approach, we simply correct all one section of the test for all the classes one day, and on another section, the next day, and so forth until all the sections of the test are covered. This often provides consistent grading in each section for each class and keeps us focused. It is such a relief when we get to the last part of the test and realize we are completely finished. Never over-promise our students when we will get something graded. Be realistic and stick with that schedule. Some teachers I have observed take one or two days after school and grade all their papers. While this may work for them, it is more advantageous to spread it over time to make it less stressful in the long run.

A fourth way to develop time management skills is to know how to respond to crises in the classroom. What is meant by this? We know that there are going to be days in the classroom where we get nothing completed because too many incidents materialize in the classroom. Be flexible with the schedule and understand this is going to "be one of those days." Trying to fix a derailed train results in frustration for all. Have you ever had fire drills occur in the middle of the period? How about students being called out alphabetically to get class pictures done for the yearbook? Or, when you have time blocked out after school to grade papers and end up with a last-minute parent meeting. Remember, how we respond in those situations says volumes to our students!

Lastly, and probably most important, learn to say no. We do want to become actively involved in the school community as a teacher, we do not want to overload ourselves to the point that we sacrifice our teaching, family, and personal responsibilities. Society applauds volunteers and those who are involved in community organizations; students are involved in many sports and clubs as well as outside social activities. Learning to prioritize breaks gives more energy to participate in the most worthwhile and/or enjoyable activities and sets a precedent and example for those around us. Rather than groaning about what we have to do, look forward to those commitments.

Procrastination

There are certainly times when you sigh and say, "I just can't face this right now," and too often, just let that task slide. One of the ways to avoid procrastination as a teacher is to develop long-term goals. We have a tendency to put off tasks that we believe are just random tasks. To avoid this problem, look at those tasks and see how they relate to the long-term goals. Recognizing the connection between those tedious tasks and how they move us forward to the end result, we will have more motivation to complete them. This takes planning and energy to complete. Set a time during the week to look at what you need to complete and make a plan to see it through. Because the struggle in the strategy is working out the plan, we could provide ourselves with an incentive for accomplishing the task. We will find that when we stick with that schedule, we will see the rewards when those tasks are completed.

Wasting time is different than time off. Teachers especially need time to do nothing. As stated earlier, quiet time in the schedule is essential. Think about how freeing it would be for us to actually schedule quiet time for ourselves. Personal time is anything that we enjoy like working out, listening to music, playing a game with your family reading a book with a plot, etc. We need to listen to our brains when it is telling us we need time; when you begin to dislike your work, become over-tired, become short with people around us, or just "out of sorts," it's time. Writing this me-time into our schedule, gives us permission to relax and will be something to look forward to on a daily basis.

Next, vary your tasks in your schedule. It takes a great amount of concentration to grade papers, prepare lesson plans, and answer emails because we are sitting in one place, being still and focused. Often we are stunned when we look up at the clock and realize how long we have been working. Just as students need to have varied activities, we also need to vary our inactive and active work and to use a different part of our brains. If we do something physical after we complete the sitting activity, we will have more motivation to complete our tasks because we feel refreshed to continue. Also, schedule an activity that does not take that much concentration. This gives your brain time to regenerate energy so that it will be ready for the next task that needs that concentration.

Finally, we need to time ourselves; we need a specific amount of time, say 15 minutes, to concentrate on a task. Get started, and before we know it, the 15 minutes are up. We will be surprised at how much we were able to accomplish. One task that I truly dislike is cleaning my classroom; seriously, I would love to have my students clean on a daily basis, but, we get caught up doing other activities, and that just does not happen. I now have put some time in my lesson planning to have the students clean their own area with antiseptic wipes and pick up wrappers off the floor. This frees up time and students feel like they are a part of the classroom.

Communicating What We Need with Our Families

Our own family, including spouses, significant others, children, and parents, need to understand what it is like to be a teacher, and to do that, we need to sit down with our families and have an in-depth conversation. Our profession is not simply an eight-hour workday, but a lifestyle throughout the school year. How should these important conversations with our family members take place?

First, literally, spend personal time writing down exactly what our expectations are for us as teachers and what support we need from our families. Remember, as we have emphasized several times in this chapter, self-care is needed. Let them know why you need downtime when you get home, even if it is just 15 minutes to relax or perhaps taking time to schedule a personal movie night, etc. It is important that we prioritize our needs, write them down, and relate to them. If it is important to commit to paper, it is important enough to discuss.

Next, find a suitable time of day to have this conversation not when someone walks through the door from the workplace or when there is a lot going on. Schedule this conversation when there are no distractions. If you have kids, make they are not playing video games or on their phones when you have this conversation. Face-to-face listening and dialogue is essential for all the stakeholders in the family.

Third, remember we are all playing for the same team; this is not a one-sided conversation, but a give and take discussion. We may need to do something for the other people in our family to accommodate the decompression time we need. Make sure that you actively listen to the others in your family so that they feel like they are heard as well. These family conferences are pivotal to family unity and harmony.

Finally, make this conversation with your family a positive experience with lots of give and take, listening and talking, and laughter and solemnity. They cannot understand our needs any more than we can understand their needs without open, honest discussion. Indeed, opening up lines of communication tells our family that they are our first priority. When we have support on our home front, we have better capacity for satisfaction in our personal life. Make time in your schedule to have this conversation. It is that important!!

Family Time vs. Professional Time

One of the last areas that we need to discuss is separating our time between family and school. It is important that one does not overshadow the other, but rather balance professional obligations. Once again, we discover why following a schedule is vital. The following tips foster this balance.

The first thing we need to do is to schedule family time, and let them know how important it is for us. Remember, our family should be our support system and not a place that provides us with more stress. Doing things together as a family should lower our stress levels and give us time to put work in the right perspective – second to our family.

Next, we need to let go of the guilt when we do not complete everything on our to-do list when spending time with our family members. Guilt only adds to the sense of failure and the stress which leads to procrastination. Who wants to do a task that has stress related to it? This is why we need to be effective time schedulers. Without distractions, get as much done on that to-do list that we scheduled for ourselves. The same principle applies to our family time; enjoy the time without distractions.

Finally and most importantly, we need to set up boundaries between the classroom and our home. For example, if we make a plan to not take any school work home, we need to honor that boundary. If we do not honor that boundary and we start taking work home, we will be stressed about interfering with our family time. Equally, taking our family issues minimizes our role as educators; students are perceptive and notice when we are distracted or bothered by something. As difficult as it can be, being able to block our outside life from intruding into the classroom is a much needed skill for a productive teacher.

To have a long, enjoyable teaching career, we need to manage and balance our time, take a lot of pride in what we do, and lessen that stress level to actually enjoy teaching. In our next chapter, we will be discussing a topic that is desperately needed today. How do we bring a successful culture back to our profession?

What Can Society Do to Make Teachers Successful?

"Success is not the key to happiness. Happiness is the key to success. If you love what you are doing, you will be successful."

— Albert Schweitzer

Overview

Since society's success is dependent on an educated workforce, one would think that our society would want our teachers to be successful. However, in the United States, teachers are not regarded as highly as in other countries. Why is this? In what ways can our society elevate the teaching profession to be more successful in the classroom? In addition to answering these questions, we will be exploring more relevant professional teacher training, increasing new teacher mentorship, changing the ways that teachers are trained to work in the classroom, receiving more support from the community, and altering the ways that teachers are evaluated.

Meaningful Teacher Training

One of the areas in that society could help us be successful is to provide meaningful professional training for the teachers and supervisory staff not just once a year, but several different in-service training opportunities throughout the school year. Most of the time we are learning state-mandated paperwork or programs that really do not help us cope with the real issues that are going on in our classroom daily. To really under-stand how to teach in the classroom requires at least a couple of years; additionally, the first four years to learning structure, curriculum, and relating to student dispositions. There are many nights when teachers are learning their curriculum, figuring out ways to deal with students who present disruptive behaviors in the classroom, and how issues like poverty, hunger, language barriers, etc affect their teaching environ-ment. Many teachers feel like failures because they feel overwhelmed and are inexperienced.

Providing seminars and training that can help us deal with these is-sues would definitely appeal to many teachers whether novices or vet-erans alike. We long to do better, meet students' needs, and improve our teaching practices because we want to improve and succeed in the classroom. Also, offering opportunities to collaborate with teachers who have had success in the classroom can provide us with the tools and ideas that have made them successful. This type of training would be more meaningful and draw more teachers because it is practical, appli-cable instruction for our routines.

If a teacher collaboration cannot be scheduled during the school year, then part of the budget should be set aside for the teachers to choose their own time to acquire the information and skills needed for their classroom struggles. There are many seminars that are offered outside the school such as online learning, behavior management, assisting sec-ond language learners or special education students, development of lesson plans, etc. There can be a course menu provided for teachers to choose from and apply budget money to attend one or two throughout the year. This can also provide teachers a way to receive credits to keep our teaching certificates up to date.

Assisting New Teachers

New teachers have the most difficult time in the classroom in their first two years to learn classroom management, a skill that instills the necessary confidence to control a classroom. If a school district cannot offer training or direction for these new teachers because of staffing or finances, then the college programs for prospective teachers should place these students in the actual environments where they can observe, learn, and practice solid classroom management techniques. By pairing a student teacher with a master teacher who has already figured out how to effectively run a classroom, the student teacher is able to learn the necessary skills and incorporate them into a learning environment. This builds confidence in the student teacher. There is nothing more defeating than being a student teacher and feeling like you are failing at what you are learning to be. Case in point, a student teacher, who was recently placed in my classroom, Mark Evans, was very willing to learn. The first two weeks that he was in my classroom were spent getting to know the students and forming relationships with them. He spent the time also learning the routine and how the classroom functioned even before he was allowed the opportunity to teach any concept in the classroom. Once the foundational relationships were established, Mark was then ready to start teaching because the students already trusted him. Once classroom relationships and routines are established, the easier it will be for the new teacher to learn the curriculum and how to effectively teach the curriculum.

Having a mentor in the school is yet another way a new teacher can flourish. When I first started teaching, I admittedly struggled. If it had not been for my mentor teachers, Brigid and Sue, I would have never lasted in teaching. Their years of experience really helped move me forward. We should take time to select capable, thriving teachers who can come along new teachers and encourage them, support them, evaluate them, guide them, and assist them throughout their first year and probably beyond that. The teachers should meet at least weekly to assess the needs of the new teacher's classroom and instruction – what is working well, what is not working well, what could be done better, and what could be done in specific scenarios. What an advantage for a new teacher to be able to speak to someone who understands what they are experiencing in the classroom. Having the mentor teacher also observe actual classroom lessons can be less intimidating to the new teacher because it is not an evaluative observation but a helpful reflection of what the teacher should change or practice. This can make a better classroom atmosphere for the new teacher because they have an advocate and supporter with their best interest at heart. The mentor teacher and the new teacher should meet with the evaluative supervisor in order to clarify what the evaluative supervisor expects when they enter the classroom.

Teacher Evaluation

Another area that should be changed for teachers to increase success in what they do is to change the way evaluations are completed. To understand how an evaluation is completed today, let's focus on an example from Pennsylvania. Pennsylvania's teachers are evaluated under the program put forth by Charlotte Danielson. This tool assesses a classroom teacher in four distinct domains: planning and preparation, the classroom environment, and instruction and professional responsibility. These domains are broken into subsections that deal with specific areas in each domain. A new teacher in PA is evaluated twice per year. A tenured teacher is evaluated once every two years. We do have walk-in visits from our administrators that do not count toward our final evaluation score, but they focus on one of the domains that they are looking at for that particular year. Let's look at how each of these domains is viewed and how this information can be used in a better way to encourage teachers.

The first domain in Charlotte Danielson's model is planning and preparation. In this domain, the evaluator is looking for knowledge or pedagogy in the subject that the teacher possesses along with the design of instruction, and student assessments. When you are a new teacher, the knowledge of what you are teaching is not complete since you are not only learning how to be an effective teacher, but you are also trying to master the information in your content area. It is unrealistic to expect that new teachers are proficient or distinctive (the highest rankings) in this area. So, it seems unfair to score them low because they do not have the experience. However, I believe this first domain is appropriate for those who have been teaching for a year or two because they have a grasp of their responsibilities. This relates to having student teachers spend quality teaching time in classroom settings where they would prefer to teach whether in a rural, suburban, or urban setting. If we have this in place the first domain would be more useful as an evaluative tool.

The second domain in the model is the classroom environment. The evaluator is looking at the overall classroom environment, managing the classroom, especially with student behavior, and organization of the physical space. This is where colleges can help student teachers be more effective. Providing examples of very effective environments where students would like to teach, having panels of experienced teachers come in and talk about their environments and discussing how they are effective in those environments would give those students a foundation to base their own classrooms on. A critical college course that should be mandated for student teachers is dealing with the gamut of disruptive behaviors in the classroom and be comprised of scenarios common in modern classrooms and methods successful teachers use to curtail these behaviors. Colleges should also address and practice how to foster relationships with the wide variety of aged children that are in our schools. This can be applied and evaluated during the time that the student teacher spends in the classroom. This will diminish a new teacher's hesitation and indecision and give them the tools and techniques to approach classroom management with confidence.

The third domain in the model addresses instruction which encompasses communicating with students, engaging students, using effective questioning methods, using different types of instruction, and assessments used in that instruction. When we go through student teaching, there are really two different kinds of models. One of the models is to be a part of two different classrooms for seven weeks each; the other model is a 14 week placement. Proponents of the first model advocate the importance for the student teacher to compare the environment and management of two different classrooms in two different settings. The other model states that the student teacher should become immersed in one classroom to establish relationships with the students and the classroom routine effectively. The first model has been around for longer and is the traditional method, whereas, the second method may be more applicable for the student teacher who knows what type of teaching environment they would prefer. This might be able to give the student teacher an opportunity to display confidence in what they can accomplish so that they are better prepared to handle their own classroom.

The fourth and final domain in the Danielson Model is professional responsibility. This domain focuses on proper documentation, reflection on teaching ability, being a part of a professional community, communicating effectively with families, and growing in a professional manner. This is certainly a responsibility that can be acquired as part of a college curriculum for teachers. What it means to be a professional, what is expected of a professional teacher, and what a professional teacher needs to do, must be clearly imprinted in the culture of prospective teachers. Again, observation and mentor-ship here by experienced teachers can teach student teachers what is expected in this domain and in their profession. It is well-said, but not always true, that perception is reality. If we are perceived as professionals, we are perceived as professionals by the public, and also the contrary is also the case. How do we want to be perceived? How we carry ourselves, how we talk, how we respond to the unexpected, and often even what we wear distinguishes us as professionals. The college course or mentor needs to look at how our society perceives a professional teacher and what criterion to avoid like social media. A deeper understanding and an exercise of professional responsibility will increase the development of professional pride and self-awareness..

Improving School Communities and the Communities that Surround Them

No matter where teachers call home, they are part of the community in which they teach. Therefore, teachers need to understand the community and how it works when they enter a new school or district. Once teachers understand how much the students and families are involved in school activities and how much the school supports the local community, we will find ways to help the community and the students that live within it.

When I entered a new school a couple of years ago, I was asked by our school activities director to be the adviser of the Key Club. I was never really an adviser to a club before, but I wanted to become part of the community. The club was floundering for a couple of years before I took over, but with good student leadership and the help from the local Kiwanis Club, we were able to find ways that the students could help the school and the surrounding community. To this day, the Key Club is very successful at raising money or holding clothing or food drives for local agencies where the school is located.

Why is it so important for a teacher to become a part of a culture within a school? One of the ways we teach our students daily is to make sure that they feel valued. This provides them an environment in which they are a vital part and can flourish. We need to do the same things as teachers. I remember one of the best things that our school had done this past year was to have teachers be a part of activities where they can have fun together. We do spend a lot of time making sure that we have activities for our students, but we should also do that for our teachers as well. During one of our previous in-service days that we had, an hour and a half of our time was used to bring teachers together to play a game of kickball, board games, volleyball, or ping pong. Not only did we work together but had fun together and enjoyed the rare opportunity to connect outside, get to know one another, and develop relationships with teachers we normally do not get to see.

When you are also a part of a culture, we tend to celebrate all our colleague's accomplishments, and they celebrate yours. The comradery trumps isolation every time. When we feel like we are isolated, we miss important events and milestones. It is no little gesture to recognize staff birthdays throughout the school year. It is no small matter when someone reaches a personal goal or earns a new degree, and we all celebrate the achievement. And, when sad events like the death of a staff member or close family member take place, how uplifting it is to support that colleague through the difficult time. It is important to have both student and staff announcements given (with permission and sensitivity) as a family deals with good and bad events that occur in their lives; we are all stakeholders and integral members of our school community. And, we must always keep in mind that we are professionals.

Uplifting the Teaching Profession

Teaching is a daily labor of love; our focus has shifted. The focus of our passion for teaching to a negative critique of our profession. Stories abound teachers that are presented in a negative light. Stories about student abuse, inappropriate behavior, social media posting, and the like deserve the negative exposure, but why is this publicized so much? There are several reasons.

The first reason is that the public has entrusted us to educate future members of our society, and to that end, we have been given a lot of power to influence the students in our classroom. The future of our country hinges on the youth of today, so we must take this awesome responsibility seriously and help guide our students to develop the knowledge and life skills that mold them into valuable members of society. Most of us remember our favorite teachers not by what they taught us, but by how they treated us in the classroom. We need to remember this responsibility on a daily basis as we frame our classroom experience for our students.

Next, we are expected to teach our students something and to have them learn something during the time they are with us. This is a difficult task for us to do because we not only have to teach curriculum but also teach character. The character is what students take with them when they move on to other classrooms and out into society when they graduate. It is important that we not only focus on what we teach, but how we teach it. We need to think about how we can influence our students daily in a positive way.

Finally, and most importantly, we must model for our students the definition of what it is to be a professional and how one acts in society. Many of our students come from different backgrounds culturally and economically need basic social knowledge that we can embed in our expectations and lessons: timeliness, punctuality, proper ways to behave, respect, courtesy, kindness, hard work, forgiveness – the list is endless. Even if our students do not achieve the goals we have set for them, at least a seed has been planted for future growth.

Hopefully, as we work our way through this chapter, we will be able to hold our profession in a more positive light. We are the ones who must hold up the torch of teaching to reveal the truth about who we are and what we do every day in the classroom. Society can support us; the negative stories are the exception, not the rule for our profession. We are an integral, influential part of the past, present, and future, and we are proud of who we do.

Our next and final chapter focuses on stories provided by many different teachers that keep them going in the good times and bad. These stories are indelibly impressed in their minds and remind them to feel positive as they share their influence. These stories reveal the joy that they have in their profession.

Magical Moments

"Miracles come in moments. Be ready and Willing."

— Dr. Wayne Dyer

Overview

My longtime friend and mentor, Tom Zsilavec, stated from the moment that he found out I was going to be a teacher, "You have the second most important job in the world behind being a parent." I have always remembered this every time I feel frustrated or unmotivated to do something. Our job is important! The daily influence that we have on our students is never truly measured because we hardly ever get to see the finished product. When you do not get to see the finished product, it is difficult to understand that you had an impact, yet, these are those moments that we never forget – those – magical moments. These are those ah-ha moments when a student understands something or maybe even comes back to tell us the difference we made in their life. Being able to experience these moments motivates us to persist during those days when we feel that we cannot go on teaching. We sometimes must be reminded that they happen to inspire us to keep going. That is what this chapter is about. Those moments that inspire us to keep going and to make that difference. These magical moments were graciously shared by professionals that I know personally.

Learning You Made a Connection

Just recently, I was in a local store purchasing clothes. As I was standing in line waiting to check out, I saw two of my former students working at two different registers. Neither of these students ever stood out in class or caused a problem, and they were both pretty good students in two separate classes. They were now both seniors; I had them the previous year. It was good to see them both have part-time jobs. As I was getting closer to the register, both students noticed that I was in line, and although they said nothing, they both acknowledged me with a wave and a smile. I got to one of the registers that neither of them was manning, but heard one of the students apologize to his customer in front of him that he did not mean to not pay attention to them but, "that is my favorite teacher down there, and I wanted to make sure that he saw me." We really never understand the connection that we make with our students until moments like this.

Liz, a former high school special education teacher at a charter school in Pennsylvania, shared a time when she had a special encounter with a former 9th grade student. As Liz was out shopping with her family at a local store, this student with her parents approached Liz and her family. The student said to Liz, "Thank you. You helped make me who I am and thank you for taking the time to help me and understand me." This student is in 12th grade this year, and Liz reports that she will be attending Penn State University in the fall of 2020. Liz said "this puts a smile on my face every time I think of it because you are never sure what kind of positive influence you have on someone unless they let you know later."

Speaking of making connections with our students, my sister-in-law, Cindy Dutt, a middle school science teacher in a suburban school district outside Pittsburgh, PA, relates that although working with students in a middle school is not an easy job, it can be very rewarding. She shared two stories with me that show the connections we make with students, but this is the one she shares the most. Cindy had an unmotivated student in her science class in 8th grade. The student had to repeat 8th grade who was repeating, but, "through focusing her attention to what her student needed the most, and her absolute love of biology, this student did pass her class". When she spoke with this student at the end of the year, the student declared she would like to become a respiratory therapist because Cindy had inspired her so much to become a scientist. The student stated that she never had a teacher that loved her subject so much and really enjoyed the way she taught the class.

Every time I think about one particular student, I feel special pride. I did not have the pleasure to teach him in my classroom, but he was the student leader of the a cappella group that I was advising. He was one of those rare students that we encounter maybe once or twice in our entire career, but we can never forget. Our high school established a college credit program where high school students were able to take college-level classes and earn transferable college credits. This student was so motivated that he had enough dual enrollment credits to earn his associate's degree at the same time he received his high school diploma. He had full scholarship offers from just about every Ivy League College that you could attend, and he chose to attend Stanford University. During his college career, he was selected to work in the travel office of the White House! This young man just graduated from Stanford University in 2020 with both his bachelor's and master's degrees. I am so proud and so inspired by his perseverance and determination that I just had to share his story. Teachers, we do make differences in our students' lives.

Jamie, a 7th grade science teacher in a suburban school district in Whitehall, Pennsylvania, shared another story about the connection that she made with one of her students. One of her former students who had been in her academic strategies classes in 7th grade stopped by to see her at an open house meet the teacher night at her school. He was about to graduate from high school during the current school year and planned to attend college. During their conversation, the student shared that he wanted to pursue a biomedical engineering degree. Jamie described this class he had taken with her as "providing ideas and ways for students to be successful in their classes." Jamie utilized science lessons to help the students understand the best practices for studying and to develop skills for solving tough problems. The student thanked her for pushing him and, because of her teaching style, he wanted to pursue science as a career. Jamie states that every time she thinks of this student, she starts to cry because of how much this moment in time meant to her. She says, "We never really know the influence you have on your students sitting in front of us until moments like this make themselves available."

Sometimes those connections we make are not apparent right away. Sharon, an elementary school teacher at a suburban school district in Emmaus, Pennsylvania, shared a story where her student showed that connection years later. Sharon was teaching in a classroom that included an autistic student who was non-verbal. He was having difficulty communicating with his teachers and peers in the classroom, although, Sharon was attempting many ways to communicate with him, and it was very frustrating for them both. One day she decided to start with a simple connection where she "used the thumbs-up to greet him and used it throughout the day to make sure that he was doing well." After this small connection with her student was made, she found herself one day in class with his head leaning on her shoulder as they were listening to a story. They have never lost this connection. Sharon saw him recently and shared that "he is older now and in high school." When she asked his current teacher if her former student would remember her, the student's current teacher stated that he has a good memory, and that she should go up to him and find out. When Sharon approached the student, the first thing he did was look at her, smile, and give her a thumbs-up. She was so taken aback that he remembered the brief moment in a classroom years ago and still maintained that connection to her.

Another story shared by Jim, a high school science teacher in both private and public schools for 43 years in Bethlehem and Allentown, PA, goes back to the quote at the beginning of the chapter from Tom Z. He explains that "he was a substitute teacher in a high school science class. I was in the community at a store and was stopped by a former student and his mother." Jim goes on to explain, "The student's father was on deployment with the Merchant Marines. He was missing the influence that his father had on him and was looking for a fatherly figure to help him during the time that his father was deployed." Jim, not really knowing the situation at the time, filled that void that his student needed. He continues, "when the student and the mother saw him in the community, they thanked him and told him how much they appreciated his help as the student was experiencing problems and was unable to approach his father about it." After serving several different communities throughout his long teaching career, this is the one story that keeps him motivated to teach to this day.

A final story to see how much of an influence we have on a daily basis when we talk about connections was shared by Christina. Christina, a high school math teacher in an urban district in Arizona and recently in Allentown, PA, experiences those moments of helping students with personal problems. One of the things she emphasized was that "the personal relationships that we make with our students makes such a difference in our day-to-day teaching." She continued to state, "This is so meaningful, especially in our urban districts in the United States; it is very important to develop those relationships with your students." The amount of trust that must be formed between student and teacher is so important for the success of the students. If the teacher can show that they can trust the students, which builds over months of time rather than days, then the student's academic productivity is increased more in that time period than if no trust had been established. She also stated that "teaching math and incorporating it into real life moments helps students understand the importance of what they are learning.

Once this is established, a light-bulb moment will take place and the motivation in the students arise."

Watching Students Evolve

When students show an understanding of the different concepts we are teaching, it reminds us of the effort and energy we invested in that light-bulb moment. This goes for both adults and students. I had the pleasure of having a student teacher, Mark Evans, this past semester. I have had some bad experiences with past student teachers, and I have had some good experiences; we never know ahead of time what your new student teacher is going to bring with them when they come to your classroom. Before this placement, I was able to meet Mark prior to his student teaching assignment with me by DeSales University. Mark was an older student teacher because this was going to be his second career. I had an established classroom culture already in place in the classrooms since the beginning of the year so introducing a new prospective teacher half-way through the year was an unknown variable. But Mark was different; he was a natural fit into the classroom very open to learning and formed a relationship with the students quickly. He was able to adapt to the routine of the classroom as well as apply and cultivate new skills that he was learning in his college classes. It was fun to watch him become progressively more proficient in the classroom as he developed ideas that he wanted to try with the students. He developed his own rhythm, and the students continued to thrive with his leadership and enjoy him as the head of the classroom. I am very proud to say that he will be a great addition to any school that he will be teaching in the future.

I had the unique pleasure of having my niece, Jennifer Mitchell, a middle school science teacher at a private school in Allentown, PA, as a student in my behavioral management class at a local community college. I have been able to watch her grow into a very special science teacher. In her young career, she has already had magical moments where she has seen her students evolve, but her most memorable one occurred when she was working with her students on projects to be displayed in her classroom. When the projects were ready to be exhibited to other classes, her students were the tour guides. Jennifer noted that "the pride that was in their faces," put a big smile on her face because she knew how much work the students put into this project. Their self-satisfaction was the product of the time and creativity she invested in planning and setting up the lessons. Seeing the result of all the work that both she and the students devoted to the success of the lesson was a truly magical moment.

Lisa Krause, an instructional supervisor at an urban high school in Allentown, PA, spent many years as an English teacher in an urban high school in Reading, Pennsylvania. She was teaching an 8th grade class at the time of this story. A student in one of her classes was particularly problematic by talking, rarely doing his work in class, and exhibiting an attitude that "was anything but pleasant." But, Lisa went the extra mile and offered him an opportunity to complete his missing classwork in her when he had a study hall period. At the end of the year, the student took the time to tell her how much he really liked her class even though he barely passed.

Fast forward ten years later when Lisa is working out at her local gym, a familiar-looking man walks by her, comes back over to greet her, and asks if she remembers him. As they were talking, they started chatting about what they had been doing for the past ten years. She learned that he had just been released from incarceration. During their conversation, the young man, the former difficult student, apologized to her for being such a bad kid in her class. He told her stories about how much he never appreciated what people were trying to do for him during his troubled teens and that he was very sorry and that he never told her that when he was in her class. Today, Lisa outside the school is a professional bodybuilder, and this former student works out with her at the gym where they were reconnected. This time he is eagerly working out with an exercise routine that Lisa suggested for him.

Those Light Bulb Moments

As teachers, we love the light-bulb moments from our students. These moments show up out of nowhere when we are teaching something or years later when a student tells us when they realized and grasped something we were teaching. Peg Shaw, a retired English teacher in an urban high school in Allentown, PA, shared a story of one of these remarkable moments. A student that she had been trying to reach academically through her lessons finally grasped what the lesson meant. For the first time in her class, "the student had what I call an "ah-ha" moment." She also states, "Once the student figured out the connection between the lesson and the subject, he became more motivated and wanted to learn more about it. Once he became more motivated, his participation increased." She concludes, "These moments can pass by quickly, so we should be on the lookout for them as we are teaching."

Working with students in a classroom day after day can become boring and stale at times. The same routine over and over, day after day, is not exactly motivating or enjoyable for either us or our students. This is why this story really is so striking. My Advanced Placement Psychology class and I decided to go outside to learn how the brain makes the connections that influence how we think. It was a cold day, and the students were shivering a little as we walked to a corner outside the school; everyone wanted to go back inside the school quickly. As I pointed to the wires and the telephone poles that were connected going up and down the street, we discussed how the wires represented our brain cells and the outside of the wires represented the myelin sheath, the protein on the outside of our cells used to transmit electrical pulses. The connections at the telephone poles represented the connections or, synapses, in our brain. One of the students standing there looked up at the pole and stated, "Mr. Dutt, my brain cells and synapses are telling me it is cold out here, and need more heat to transmit my impulses!" Not only did I laugh for days after this, but knew she grasped the connection well enough to later receive a 100% on the unit test. That light shined brighter when the brain cells were challenged in that cold weather.

Fun and Emotional Stories That We Never Forget

As this book is being written, our whole world of teaching has changed. We are amid a worldwide pandemic of the Corona virus. It has changed the way traditional teaching is being utilized and brought it to its knees. We are searching for ways to communicate with our students, and it has not been easy because all of us do not have the technology to reach out to every one of our students. We keenly miss our students and scrambling to keep up our communications with them as we learn how to teach online. Gabby Auvil, a teacher who taught 8-year-olds in Philadelphia and now 4th grade in Nashville, TN, was reaching out to her students to check on their social-emotional well-being. She states, "I was able to get a hold of 10 out of her 30 students using the online program Zoom." She was speaking to them about the best and worst parts about school being closed for the last month. Gabby thought that "her students would say that they love getting up late or being at home." She was surprised to hear that the kids "liked seeing their classmates on the Zoom call, and also missed not being at school." This comment encouraged and inspired her for the rest of the school year. Even though we are challenged in the classroom and face challenging times, we can never forget what we do and why we do it.

There is nothing in the teacher manuals that dictate against having fun with our students. I had the pleasure of speaking to 14 different early education and elementary school teachers and retired principals in the East Penn School District and other private schools in eastern Pennsylvania. One of the stories that the group shared with me was a time the two elementary school teachers were standing in the hallway in between class periods. The teachers had planned a snow-themed day and decided to have fun. We are all taught in college that we must keep a professional image with not only our students, but also, with the community at large. A lot of times, we see our teachers as not really having fun at their jobs. They were using white yarn balls and cotton balls to use as snow in their classrooms, so when they heard the students coming down the hall, they were armed and ready as the students rounded the corner. The teachers "pelted" the students with the yarn balls and cotton balls. For the next couple of minutes, the students and the teachers threw the cotton balls at each other with lots of laughter; the incident has never been forgotten because the students talk about it all the time. These are moments that are easily overlooked; these are moments that make the teachers look real; these are moments when authentic learning begins.

Finally, we have one unforgettable story, and emotional story relayed by Kelli Rocchi, a music teacher and choral director at a suburban high school in Nazareth, Pennsylvania. We met at a local a cappella festival that I was directing. Kelli's girl a cappella group, the Nightingales, had a chance to perform at Carnegie Hall in New York City. They were all excited about this opportunity since very few groups can perform at this iconic venue. As they were preparing to leave to perform, Kelli shared, "there was a snow/ice storm that was predicted for the weekend that they were to perform. The governor was also considering a travel ban in response to the upcoming storm because the weather was supposed to turn bad quickly." Of course, Kelli and the Nightingales were upset about the prospect of not being able to go perform. She continues, "I received a call from my principal who told me that the district had allocated specific funds for the group to cover hotel rooms closer to Carnegie Hall." Kelli said, "this was most magical for me because she was able to conduct The Nightingales on the stage of Carnegie Hall in front of a large crowd. It was one of the most emotional and proudest moments of my teaching career."

These stories and more keep us talking about our jobs in a positive light. We do have many challenges to face on a daily basis, but I hope sharing these stories and the different information provided in this book gives us hope as we teach the students that will be leading our country in the future. The famous song, "We Are the World," states at the beginning that, "there comes a time when we heed a curtain call." Our call is to make a difference in the lives of those we teach. Our call is to bring that thought and enthusiasm to the classroom. Our call is to inspire those with who we are connected – in our home, classroom, and community. May this book inspire you to begin or continue our professional journey ad teachers with passion, enthusiasm, and pride.

Appendix

Below is a copy of the questions that I used to interview the many teachers who contributed information for this book. Not all the information was used in writing this book, but it was used as a framework to set it up. Thank you to all the teachers that helped make the writing of this book possible.

Interview Questions for Book on Modern Teaching

1. What is your name?

2. What is the subject(s) you teach or job performed in school?

3. Years in teaching or working in education:

4. Do you work in rural, suburb, or urban setting?

5. What is your overall view of modern education?

6. What inspired you to be involved in education?

7. Working in education, what are or were some issues that you encountered on a daily basis? How did you deal with those challenges?

8. What types of skills should a person possess if they want to work in a school setting in our modern society?

9. What advice would you provide someone who is struggling in our modern classrooms to improve their situation?

10. How can our society start recruiting people to become teachers for the future?

11. Have you had any magical moments after you started teaching? What were they and how were they magical?

12. If you could go back and change anything from the time you started teaching what would that be?

13. Name three essential skills that would benefit modern teachers or people who work in education today.

14. How can educators balance time between school and family to be effective in today's society?

15. How can teachers communicate effectively with families and the communities that they serve?

16. What types of discipline are most effective in the classroom?

17. What can college programs provide potential teachers that would help them become successful in the modern classroom?

18. How can families help teachers to be more effective with their children in the classroom?

19. How can communication between administration and faculty be improved to make schools more effective?

20. Are there any additional comments that you would like to make to enhance the teaching experience in our modern classrooms?

*Thank you so much for your participation in this survey.

Acknowledgments

I have been told by many people that writing a book is not easy. You were all right, but this journey was totally worth it! None of this would have been possible without the continued encouragement from my wife, Nancy. You have encouraged just about everything that I come up with including this book. Thank you for being there every day to help me become the person that I am today!

I would have been unable to write this book without my teaching mentors, Brigid and Sue. You both saw something in me that you molded and gave me the courage to do something that I would have never thought I would be able to do, teach.

A special thank you to all my colleagues in the teaching field who took time out of their busy schedules and sat through the interview process for this book. Without your knowledge and deep commitment to this profession, this book would have not been possible.

Thank you to both of my editors, Tina Larson and Lori Handelman. You took the concept of this book and helped make it into something special. God has blessed you with talents that do not go unnoticed.

To all my students past and present, thank you for helping to mold me into the teacher I am today. I know that there were ups and downs on that journey with you, but you have given me a chance to do something that I really love.

A special thank you to the Allentown School District and Keith Falko for taking a chance on a person who never taught before and gave him an opportunity to show what he could do in the classroom. For that, I am eternally grateful!

Finally, a special thank you to Mary, Lisa, Sam, and Ken for critiquing this work.

About the Author

Jeffrey Dutt received his Bachelor's Degree in Social Work from Mansfield University of Pennsylvania in 1990. He then received his Master's Degree in Special Education from Lehigh University in 1993. After a 12-year professional career in Social Work, he has enjoyed a 20-year career as a Special Education and History teacher in the Allentown School District in Allentown, PA and a 17 year career as an Adjunct Professor in the Education Department at Lehigh Carbon Community College in Schnecksville, PA.

In 1990, while attending Mansfield University, he was awarded the Outstanding Student Service Award and was proud to receive the Best Special Education Teacher Award from his students in 2011.

He currently lives in Emmaus, PA with his wife, Nancy. They have been married for 27 years.

HISTRIA

BOOKS

A Tale of Two Villains
THEME AND SYMBOLISM IN
Dracula and the Harry Potter Saga
Calvin Cherry

RANDY O'BRIEN
GETTYSBURG BY MORNING

VLAD DRACULA
The Life and Times of the Historical Dracula
KURT W. TREPTOW

NETWORKS RISING
THINKING TOGETHER IN A FLATTER WORLD
CHRISTOPHER BURNS

The Lost Diary of GEORGE WASHINGTON
The Revolutionary War Years
JOHNNY TEAGUE

LUCREZIA Borgia
FERDINAND GREGOROVIUS

FOR THESE AND OTHER GREAT BOOKS VISIT

HISTRIABOOKS.COM